Praying for Healing while Planning a Funeral

A MIRACULOUS STORY OF HOPE

ROSEY BRAUSEN

BroadStreet
PUBLISHING

BroadStreet Publishing Group, LLC
Racine, Wisconsin, USA
www.broadstreetpublishing.com

Praying for Healing while Planning a Funeral
A MIRACULOUS STORY OF HOPE

Cover design by Chris Garborg at www.garborgdesign.com
Typesetting and interior design by Katherine Lloyd at www.TheDESKonline.com

Stock or custom editions of BroadStreet Publishing titles may be purchased in bulk for educational, business, ministry, fundraising, or sales promotional use. For information, please e-mail info@broadstreetpublishing.com.

Printed in China

15 16 17 18 19 20 7 6 5 4 3 2 1

Contents

God's will
is to heal disease, but we
live on a fallen planet and
we may go home through
the pathway of illness.
The trick is to love Him so
recklessly in the process
that you leave nothing
on the table when asking
for healing except His
sovereignty.

Introduction

Praying for healing is a tricky business. It's a kaleidoscope of hope, doubt, belief, faith, trust, and fear all wrapped up together. Throw in some feelings of unworthiness, confusion about God's sovereignty, too much Internet information, plus all that comes with not feeling well, and you have a perfect storm, a true spiritual battleground. It just so happens to be the place where my husband, Gary, and I found ourselves on March 15, 2011.

Have you seen the movie *The Avengers?* The earth's superheroes have to team together to take on a fierce villain who wants to control humanity. It's not easy to save the earth. The heroes really have to duke it out in order to win. My favorite scene is at the end when all the Avengers are sitting in a destroyed diner; their clothes are dusty and torn. They are covered in scrapes and bruises. Frankly, they are exhausted and all they want is a sandwich and a cold drink. This is how Gary and I felt as we journeyed through cancer. We joined God in a fierce battle for Gary's life because we believed that God is the author of our first day and our last—not cancer. However, we don't have superpowers. We are ordinary people, who live ordinary lives, and have ordinary jobs. But it is what happened to us through the journey of cancer that makes our story so extraordinary.

As you read our story, it is important to remember that

in the Bible Jesus didn't heal the same way twice; some of the healings were immediate, while others were a process. Each biblical healing has specific attributes especially designed for the person He healed, as well as to teach the world how He longs for a relationship with us. As Gary and I went through our journey together, God was faithful to bring these stories to our minds, encouraging us along the way. They taught us the way we should go, and how we should respond to Him in our situation. He lavished us with patience, mercy, and love as He opened up His healing miracles to us. We used these stories as our pathway out of cancer. Like the healings in the Bible, He may speak to you or your loved one in a completely different way, so it is important to leave room for the creative God to dazzle and surprise you.

Another part of our story, which is a little harder to understand, is that we believe that because God is so relational, because He loves us so much, and because when Jesus died He sent the Holy Spirit to dwell within us, He communicates with us all day long. We believe that He speaks to us through Scripture; or He speaks to us from a note from a friend, or during our dreams at night…really, in a thousand different ways. You may be thinking, "Sure, this is plausible," but by the end of our story my prayer is that you know this to be the truth and your desire to get to know our loving God in new ways is undeniable. He loves you tremendously, endlessly, fully, and completely, and He longs for you to discover His amazing love.

We get it. God seems so far out there, so intangible, so busy. "Does He really want to talk to me when He has so many things on His plate? After all, there are starving people in Africa, genocide wiping out thousands of people in other countries, collapsing governments, and billions of prayers for Him to tend to every day. How can He possibly be so tender, loving, and omniscient to be aware of all that and still communicate with me individually?" These were actually many of Gary's own questions for most of our twenty years of marriage, so don't feel bad if you are unsure about the validity of communicating with God. He knows you. He knows where your limits are, and He will reveal Himself to you as you are ready.

One request we have is for you to keep an honest log of your emotions as you read this story, which can be done in a separate notebook, or you can write in the margins of this book. Make note of the aspects of our story that make you angry, defensive, sad, frustrated, hopeful, peaceful, or joyful. We ask this because in these emotions are hidden self-secrets, the beauty of your heart, wounds, and the sins you struggle with that all need to be worked out with God. He is tender toward your journey. He understands your disappointments, loneliness, heartache, and trust level. His heart is to heal you emotionally, spiritually, and physically. He wants to set you free, not because you have enough faith, and not even because you are worthy enough. But He wants to heal you because it's His nature to do so and He is God. Go figure.

The kicker, and what brings us all to our knees, is that this book will not be able to explain the fact that many people more devout and obedient than Gary have prayed for healing and have gone home through the pathway of illness. We can't even begin to address this reality in the pages contained here.

We are here to simply tell you our story—the way God chose to move in our lives, and deal with us. And by you reading the way God chose to deal with us, we pray that our story brings you hope, increases your faith, and stirs a desire in you to trust yourself with our wonderful God. He lavishly loves you and He desperately wants to help you into healing, whether it is spiritual, emotional, mental, or physical.

Jesus promised us, "And you will know the truth, and the truth will make you free" (John 8:32). May God reveal truth to your heart as you read the pages of this book, and may you walk in a greater level of freedom and intimacy with God than ever before.

Family picture prior to Gary's diagnosis

Chapter 1

It's Just a Virus

Gary was born on September 17, 1960, in St. Paul, Minnesota. He is the middle son of Shirley and Donovan Brausen, and a true scrapper by nature—he likes this about himself. He likes to work hard and he loves a good challenge. Both athletic and disciplined, he loves to shoot the puck around or, as he says, "put the biscuit in the basket." This is hockey lingo.

In April of 2010, Gary ran an aggressive nine-mile race through the hilly terrain of Hyland Park. In September of the same year, he turned fifty and celebrated by participating in a duathlon with his friend Scott. He also increased his 6:30 a.m. hockey game with work colleagues to two mornings per week.

The next month he caught a nasty cold. It cleared pretty quickly—nothing to worry about, or so we thought. In November the cold was back but cleared again. The end of December brought the return of that persistent cold, so he finally went to the doctor to try and find out what was wrong—why was this cold continually coming back? The doctor didn't think too much of it, believing it was just a virus or the remains of seasonal allergies.

By mid-January, however, Gary's energy was dropping, he was losing weight, and sleep was impeded by a persistent dry cough. He decided to stop playing hockey and running our youngest son's hockey practices until his energy came back. In late February, he went to the doctor again, but this time as he was leaving the doctor's office, a stern voice in his head prompted him to request a a chest X-ray. When the radiologist reviewed the X-ray, they found pneumonia—finally a diagnosis. But by early March the aggressive antibiotic wasn't working and the cough was not only persisting but getting worse. His doctor didn't want to wait the typical four weeks and ordered another chest X-ray. The pneumonia was still present in his lower left lung, so his doctor ordered a chest CT scan.

It all seems so clean and tidy when I write it this way— yes, nice and orderly. First, a persistent cold, then we think it's pneumonia…no, it's not pneumonia; it must be something else. But the truth is that while we were engaged with our busy lives, cancer had entered our house like a thief in the night, pulled up a chair, and had joined us for dinner. And we didn't even know we had a houseguest.

Somehow, slowly over time we had accepted Gary's deteriorating state as somewhat normal. He was keeping up his typical athletic pace but it was taking him longer and longer to regain his energy for the next day. His mood had altered; he was more pensive and generally preoccupied.

I picked up the slack, and some resentment, like a vacuum. As he went through boxes of Kleenex, I surprised myself with the amount of excuses I could make for my husband's changing behavior. Our life, though very normal on the outside, was boiling over on the inside.

Finally, Skip, Gary's friend and coworker, stopped him in the hall. "Dude, I have to tell you the truth," he said, "you look like complete crap." Skip's candor sent Gary straight into the bathroom to take a long, hard look at himself in the mirror. He thought, "I look like I'm dying." But never in his wildest imagination did he think it was true.

GOD LEADS THE WAY

If you have ever spent any time in the Bible, you would be quick to notice how gracious God is to His people. Time after time, He chooses the weakest characters to show His glory and His majesty. It's not very flattering to speak about, but Gary and I fit this description. We were unprepared for cancer—we could have easily been lost in it except for the fact that God was faithful to make our pathway out of illness clear. He did this in a vast array of signs, wonders, prayers, Scriptures, and conversations.

One of the reasons I trust God implicitly is because He is a God who doesn't change (Malachi 3:6). He is absolutely consistent with who He says He is and how He has always revealed Himself to be. This means that the God who parted the Red Sea, sent the magi to Jesus, and raised Lazarus from the dead, is the same God who wants to be in a relationship with you and me. And when we invite Him into our heart, He brings all His godliness with Him. His favor rests on us. It's the best hostess gift we will ever receive in our entire lives.

God also considers being in relationship with you to be priceless. He treasures you and your vulnerabilities so completely that He will hold Himself back lest He overpowers you.

He allows you to come into a deeper and deeper relationship with Him in your own time, gently prodding you along the way. Yet He is the One who is God.

God knows each and every one of His beloved children, and He loves to delight in each one individually. He knows you better than you know yourself, and because of this He cares for you in the most sensitive ways. Every relationship needs communication, and being in relationship with God is no different. He will speak to you in dreams and visions, signs and wonders, a phrase that catches your ear and sits in your spirit, a passage of Scripture, or even through a song. So if you listen to what He is speaking, He is faithful to answer your prayers, bring you comfort and direction, or even prepare you for a life-altering event.

In August of 2010, just six months before the diagnosis would come, and while Gary was still feeling terrific, our neighbors Fred and Janet joined us in our front yard for a little chat. They were eager yet hesitant to share their story with us. It was actually a sit-down-and-stay-a-while kind of story. And we could tell by their nonverbals that they were unsure of how we would respond.

Fred and Gary are both engineering managers and had a few meetings together for a brief time in 2008. Engineers and managers at that time were required to keep notes of all their meetings. These notebooks are usually the property of the company they work for, but in many cases these notebooks are lost or destroyed as projects finish. Fred was of the engineer variety that kept all of his notebooks throughout the years. Newly retired, he was anxious to burn them. Fred thought that on an average he probably used four notebooks per year for thirty years.

As Fred was telling us his story, he was being very precise about the details, how big the fire was, how hot it became, and how long it burned, making sure we understood the amount of notebooks that were being burned and how many possible pages they contained. He then explained that he thought Gary's name might have been on about three pages at the most.

Fred told us that this massive fire burned for about seven hours before it finally died down. There was absolutely nothing left of the notebooks except dust, ash, and one small white piece of paper that was not burned at all except for around the edges. Fred was immediately drawn to the paper that was embedded in the ash. He looked at us right in the eye, drawing us deeply into his story. Then he said, "I am not sure what this means, but it means something. Statistically, this isn't possible. All the paper was burned. It burned for hours. My 2008 notebooks were in the middle stacks, and there was absolutely nothing left of any notebook except this!"

He handed the paper to Gary and my stomach flip-flopped. There it was: Gary's name as clear as could be in the center of small slightly singed piece of paper. It wasn't until later that we understood the significance of this sign. For now, Gary graciously took the small slip of paper, pondered it for moment, and then put it into his drawer when he went back into the house. He would later tell me that this little sign completely freaked him out and that as soon as he saw his name he started to sweat profusely. The months wore on and we continued with life.

A sign for Gary that he was going to survive the fire

MY JOURNEY TOWARD GOD

In the Bible Jesus often talks about the need to be born again in order to fully understand His lordship and have eternal life. It's a radical idea to grasp, and one that even the biblical characters struggled to understand at times with Jesus explaining it to them in person.

Needless to say, I struggled with this concept for years. I had grown up Catholic; my dad was a deacon of the Catholic Church who made sure our home was a rich environment of theological discussion. My mom loved to relate to God through service, constantly lending a hand to others in need, even when she was more than exhausted raising her own ten children. Theoretically, I could talk good Bible, I knew God was God and Jesus was His Son, and I loved to serve others, so I thought I was good to go.

As I became a mom myself in 1997, my desire to know God in a new way was undeniable. Who was this God who knit my boys together in my womb? Who was this God who had blessed me with such abundance? I liken my experience to when I was given a handful of M&M's when I was a kid. I loved the M&M's I was given—they were colorful, rich, and satisfying, yet they had to come from somewhere. Where was the rest of the bag of M&M's, and, more importantly, who was holding the bag?

In October of 2000 I realized that the rest of the bag of M&M's was in the hand of Jesus. I had been living my life with Jesus in my head. I knew all the right answers, but I had not opened up my heart to the possibility of having a one-on-one relationship with our living God. Some would want to blame this on religion, and for a while I was also in this camp—so many rules and laws, and way too many hypocrites.

God would later heal me of this blaming nature though. The reality was harder to accept. I was given many opportunities to open up my heart to the Lord, but I never did. I kept God in my intellect where it was safe—where I could think about Him and know about Him without Him getting too involved in the details of my life. Embracing a truly living God who opened up the secrets of Scripture to me, who desperately wanted to heal my wounds, and grow me in ways unimaginable, was hard to accept. This was especially true since this kind of relationship was going to go beyond Sunday and enter into my every thought, action, and word.

God was meeting me in my heart, in the midst of the good, the bad, and the ugly. He was a God who walked me through the mundane and into the fabulous, all of which are equally important to Him. For a long time I called my transition an "activation" of my faith. Truthfully, I had become a born-again Christian and was uncomfortable with the connotations of this phrase. Yep, I also harbored a whole lot of judgment against those born-again Christians. But as I came to know the Lord in new ways, I prayed that Gary would "activate" his faith too.

GARY'S SIGNIFICANT STEP TOWARD GOD

We attended a nondenominational church called Evergreen, and for whatever reason Gary was hearing the gospel in a new way there. He was intrigued, and for the first time in his life the Bible was making sense to him. At Evergreen, they have a huge wooden cross for people to nail their name to when they have accepted Jesus into their heart as their Savior and Lord. In July of 2009 Gary nailed his name to that cross. And in January of 2011 he nailed his name to that cross a second time because the first time he wasn't really "all in."

When Gary came to the Lord the second time, that's when things really began to change. My strong-minded, intellectual husband was more tender than he had ever been before. He was curious about the journey the boys and I were on. He was willing to ask for prayer, and he was becoming more vulnerable. That might be a little too strong, so for now let's just say he was more approachable and intrigued about having a relationship with God.

Winter of 2011 pressed on, as did Gary's deteriorating health. The night before Gary's February doctor's appointment, he asked for prayer. "Rosey, my throat is so irritated," he said. "Will you place your hand on my throat and pray for me?"

Are you kidding me? I had been praying for such a request for nine years. In a New York minute I was at his side with my hand "gently" on his throat. As we prayed, my hand moved to his lower left lung. The room was heavy with the presence of the Holy Spirit. I repeated to Gary what the Holy Spirit spoke into my heart, "Gary, you will need to walk in your healing. I have walked Rosey ahead of you for this purpose. Lean on what I have taught her, and then she will need your prayer."

We had no idea what to make of those words. Why had my hand moved down to his lower left lung anyway? Gary took "walk in my healing" as a directive, but how? For my part I really didn't like the last line. Why would I need Gary's prayers too?

THE DIAGNOSIS

In early March of 2011, our doctor ordered a CT scan. It came back with odd results. There was a milky substance in Gary's lower left lung, something akin to pneumonia. We were sent to a pulmonologist, who had Gary go through a variety of breathing exercises, and when the testing was complete, he met with us to discuss the results.

He said, "Now, if you weren't sitting in front of me, I would say these are the results of a very sick man, but you look great and your lungs sound clear. There have been a lot of odd lung infections going around this year. Let's get a biopsy and see what course of antibiotics will do the trick to clear this infection up."

This news sounded good to us—at least it was something that could be taken care of by simple antibiotics. We wanted to get those antibiotics pumping so Gary could finally kick this thing. Gary and I went home that day, glad to have an opportunity to identify the culprit more precisely.

A week later, as Gary was in the recovery room after the biopsy, his doctor stopped by to discuss how the procedure had gone. He told us he was able to get a great sample from the mass and they should be able to have an answer in a few days as to what it was. Needless to say, we were elated. Normalcy was on the horizon and we just had a few more days to wait.

"What are you looking for?" I asked.

"Fungal infections, basically," he replied. "And we will also need to rule out cancer." Gary's eyes were opening and closing like he had tacky glue on his eyelids. "Are his eyes typically this yellow?" the doctor asked.

Umm, hadn't I noticed in the last week or two a yellow tint to his skin and eyes? However, it wasn't the tint of Gary's eyes that made my heart hit the floor. It was the way the doctor looked at me when he said the word *cancer*. I can't explain it. I just knew something was wrong. I thought the doctor knew too, but when asked later he said he had no indication that cancer would be found. A quick glance at Gary told me he was completely oblivious to what the doctor said. I attributed his lack of concern to still coming out of anesthesia. Gary later said he never even heard him utter the word.

They took Gary into another room, and I went down to the cafeteria to process my reaction. I don't remember much about my meal, but I was acutely aware of all the people in the cafeteria that day. What burdens were they carrying? How did I look to them? At this point in my relationship with the Lord,

I knew what my physical response meant. I sat there praying for strength and hope that I was wrong.

Gary and I went home later that day. We both went back to work, and for the next two days life returned to normal. When the call came at 2:57 p.m. on March 15, Gary was at home by himself. The doctor said, "Gary, I have some very bad news for you. You have lung cancer."

Gary doesn't remember asking the doctor any questions. He doesn't even remember the rest of the conversation or that he was taking notes of what the doctor told him. As he hung up the phone, his knees buckled, and he slid down the wall. How does an athletic, nonsmoking fifty-year-old man get lung cancer? The irony is that our neighbor Mark, who is the chief pathologist of our hospital, just happened to be the one to work on Gary's biopsy. We found ourselves in his living room three hours later.

Our neighbors Mark and Pat had been our mentors since we moved into the neighborhood fifteen years earlier. Roughly ten years older than us, they are the kind of people you immediately like. They are salt-of-the-earth people—natural, honest, caring, hardworking, and wonderfully unassuming. They are both pillars of compassion. We have watched them care for their older children and their parents, and they have watched us manage marriage and our young boys. But now Mark was telling us about Gary's cancer over a beer.

Mark was sitting in his chair, Pat was across the room knitting a blanket that she would later give to Gary, and Gary and I were sitting together on the couch. Mark began to explain what he saw in Gary's biopsy. He told us that typically cancer will consolidate itself into a tumor, but what Gary's biopsy revealed was that this cancer was living in his vascular lining of his lung rather than "tumoring up," hence the appearance of pneumonia. None of this was good news. The cancer was behaving oddly. We could tell by the severity of Mark's demeanor that we were in for a tough fight. We asked that horrible question: "How long?" He thought one year, maybe two years—tops.

How do you explain someone's reaction when they hear they only have a year or two to live? Gary pressed Mark for more information, desperately seeking anything that would give him hope. Finally, with every possible question exhausted, Gary looked at me and then lowered his eyes to the floor. There was such a mixture of shock and sadness in his eyes. Is this really happening to us? My mind screamed, "Lord, we need help!"

I took Gary's face in my hands and said, "Gary, look at me, honey. We serve a mighty and fearful God who loves to heal people. He hasn't spoken yet. Miracles happen every day. Gary, God will help us fight this cancer."

Gary heard what I said, but I could see the despair in his eyes. The look in his eyes that night bored deep into my soul. How was I going to be able to help him through this journey into victory? My spirit cried out to the Lord: "Lord, I'm trusting that You are God and You change not. Please, still be the God of all healing! We are in desperate need of Your provision."

We left Mark and Pat's with Mark's wisdom in our ears: "We all come to the end of our days. For you, Gary, the question is, what are you going to do with the time that remains?"

We heard what he said with ours ears, but taking in the information as truth was a long time in coming. We held hope that perhaps it wasn't so bad. More testing would give us more information, and possibly more hope…right?

That evening for me was the beginning of many silent-tear nights, nights when after the boys and Gary were asleep, my processing and prayers would begin. And without fanfare or acknowledgment, silent tears would find their way down my cheeks, the sum total of the day's events, emotion brought to service in tangible form. "Lord, our boys! Please, sweet Jesus, You have to help us tell Bennett and Alec."

We decided to wait until Friday before we would tell them anything.

TELLING OUR BOYS

In preparation for telling Bennett, who was thirteen at the time, and Alec, who was ten years old, Gary and I thought it would be a good idea to get them Live Strong bracelets from Lance Armstrong's cancer foundation. In retrospect, it makes me laugh at the absurdity of it all. We were about to tell our boys that their strong, healthy, nonsmoking dad had lung cancer and we thought yellow bracelets would somehow help. OK, they actually did help as we went through the process, but at that moment there was nothing that was going to make this discussion any easier.

Every family has a special dynamic that makes them a family. For some it's a shared interest in sports, or cooking, or perhaps even reading together. For our little family, it is conversation. We talk about everything: no topic is off limits;

no emotion is too raw to discuss. Our family is a safe place to air our dirty laundry or our greatest success. This has both its ups and its downs. I pray that my future daughters-in-law are not expecting the strong, silent type of male. Strong my boys are, but silent they are not.

I don't know why this is our dynamic. Gary likes to yank my chain and say I am to blame. He says that even our animals are emotionally extroverted. This makes me laugh, especially when he is holding court in our kitchen gregariously telling us about the daily antics of being an engineer. If someone can make engineering comical, you have a true example of the pot calling the kettle black.

As for Bennett and Alec, they are a quirky mix of both of us, and then so much more. They are witty, athletic, intelligent, hardworking, caring kids. Bennett is thoughtful, wise, honest, discerning, and relational. Alec is direct, passionate, determined, softhearted, and curious. They are our joy, and up to this point in their lives they were living a dream. As Bennett would come to say, life was perfect until cancer almost destroyed everything.

Alec has since said he knew immediately that something was wrong when I picked them up from school that day, which makes complete sense to me. We were about to blow their world apart, and, as the hour was quickly approaching, my tough veneer was peeling away. Thankfully, Bennett was busy talking to his carpool buddy and didn't really pick up on my mood. When we got home, Alec saw his dad sitting on the couch in the middle of the day and knew he and Bennett were going to be in big trouble.

"Come on, boys," Gary said, "we need to have a family meeting. We have something to talk to you about." Alec and Bennett immediately started a nervous sort of fidget, indicative of kids who might just have a few stories to tell us when they are twenty-seven and thirty years old. They exchanged a fearful glance of solidarity and suspicion that makes me now laugh—a look that said, "Boy, are we going to get it! How did they know? Did *he* tell? Wait a minute…what did we do?"

I said, "Guys, we have something very difficult to tell you. We don't know how or why, but the reason your dad has been feeling so sick is because he has lung cancer." It was a direct shot to their hearts. If I had to do it again, I would have rehearsed the delivery first, because a little less direct would have been beneficial here. But I really didn't know how else to tell them, so I just got to the point quickly.

Bennett was off the couch and on his feet. "What?" he exclaimed. "When did you find out?"

"Well, we found out three days ago, but we didn't have a lot of information and we wanted to wait until the weekend to tell you," I said. "Then you would have some time to process this information before going back to school on Monday."

"Mom, how could you keep this from us for three days?" exclaimed Alec. "He's our dad and we should have been praying for him!" It would be the first of many times that our boys' faith would lift us up and over a hurdle.

"Well, we needed to figure things out," I replied, a little taken back at how disgruntled they were for not being included immediately. "The important thing is that we have to help Dad fight. We will need to pull together as a family like never before. Dad is going to need our help to get well."

Gary gave each boy a bracelet and said, "I'm going to beat this thing. Will you guys help me?"

Quiet nods of agreement came from each boy. What was I expecting? A Hollywood-scripted response? Hugs? Tears? I don't know, but definitely something more than head nods. Maybe I have watched way too many cheesy Hallmark movies to know how these conversations should have gone.

Ben and Alec prior to diagnosis (ages 13 and 10)

SEEKING GOD

Hear, O LORD, when I cry with my voice, and be gracious to me and answer me. When You said, "Seek My Face," my heart said to You, "Your face, O LORD, I shall seek" (Psalm 27:7–8).

Gary and I had no plan for what to do after we told the boys. Why hadn't that occurred to us before that point? The only thing I could think of was to run—run as fast as we could. The North Shore had always been our family's retreat place. We love Lake Superior and all it has to offer. It was 4:00 p.m. on Friday but miraculously I was able to find a cabin. So we threw some things into a bag and within forty-eight minutes after our "family meeting" we were headed to Duluth and hopefully some good distraction.

The car ride didn't contain much conversation about cancer. It was beginning to sink in slowly, but as night fell and Gary's coughing spells increased, it was impossible to ignore. Plus, just our luck, in Duluth there must have been some sort of lung cancer awareness drive going on, because we saw about five different TV commercials on how lethal lung cancer can be. Seriously, it was not funny.

We were trying to escape lung cancer for just a little while and it was plastered all over the TV in Duluth. Not to mention the commercials were telling us that only 16 percent of lung cancer patients actually survive. We couldn't find the clicker fast enough to change the channel when those commercials came on. Eventually, however, Gary tried to get some sleep and the boys and I sat curled up on the couch.

Sitting alone with the boys that night in the cabin, the gravity of Gary's illness hit me. Was this what it would be like? Just the two boys and me, all alone, for the rest of our lives? My whole spirit lurched at the thought. "Lord, how are we supposed to do this?" I asked Him again.

With Gary's coughing as our backdrop, the boys and I prayed into the night. Alec was on his knees for about an hour and a half, while Bennett was deep in the Word. Finally, exhaustion hit them both and sleep was a sweet diversion.

My prayer time was just beginning as the boys drifted

off for the night. I had a lot of wrestling to do with the Lord. Biblical stories were swirling in my head—the requests of the persistent widow before the judge, Abraham's request for Sodom and Gomorrah, and the ability to move mountains if I just believed. These Scriptures and many more were like rapid fire in my brain. And even though every bone in my body cried out for a miracle, my spirit sought my heavenly Father in His throne room.

In complete honesty and surrender, I prayed—OK, I actually sobbed: "Lord, You know what I want. You know the prayers and fears of my heart, but, Lord, what is Your plan? Whatever it is, I will walk it out to the best of my ability and You will always stay my God. But, Lord, I need to know, because if You are going to take Gary home, I need to know how to help him through the process. But if You are going to heal him, I have no idea what You need from us." My heart wrenched as I gave the whole situation to the Lord.

I can't really describe that moment of prayer. I have never felt anything like it before that time, nor have I felt anything like it to this day. It was naked and raw, peaceful and pure. It had the softness of utter surrender and the grit of uncensored trust. It was akin to helplessness, yet it was full of courage.

What was God's response to my intense heartfelt prayers? Nothing. There was complete silence. My God who speaks so lovingly to me all day long was completely silent on the issue. I waited. Exhaustion hit, I helped Gary through another coughing attack, and then noticed that Alec was sleeping but fitfully. I laid down beside him and softly whispered words of reassurance into his ear, then sleep came for me too.

Chapter 2

Faith through Forgiveness

Often the Lord chooses the moments before we fully wake to speak with us through His Holy Spirit. It is the time that cannot be described as either sleep or wakefulness. I can only speak of it as a suspension of reality. It is in this time that I understand John 16:13 the best: "But when He, the Spirit of truth, comes, He will guide you into all the truth; for He will not speak on His own initiative, but whatever He hears, He will speak; and He will disclose to you what is to come."

As I was entering this place the next morning, my mind was full of Scripture about God's will to heal disease. Scripture after Scripture continued to roll through my mind. I wish I had been more awake so I could have written them all down, but the one Scripture I remembered was Jeremiah 30:17: "For I will restore you to health and I will heal you of your wounds." That was my answer.

I bounded out of bed and ran to Gary. He was still sleeping. I hesitated for at least half a second, and then woke him up. "Gary, God is going to heal you!" I declared. "God is going to heal you! His will is to bind your wounds and heal your diseases." I was like a maniac.

Then I said, "Let's go for a walk—we have to talk."

"What? Rosey it's got to be six o'clock and it's freezing outside. The cold air is going to make my cough worse. "

"It's actually six thirty," I said. "Come on, we have to talk and we have to get started now. We have to talk about some things and it can't wait—plus, the boys can't hear what we need to discuss. God's going to heal you and we have to get our hearts ready!"

I still can't believe he pulled himself out of bed and into his winter clothes, which is such a pure example of how quickly obedient Gary became to walk out what the Lord would have for him. This was just the beginning of the fight he would exhibit, but we didn't know that yet. Thankfully, the morning wasn't bitter cold and for Duluth the wind was mild.

On our walk, Gary and I went through the equivalent of three years of marriage counseling in about fifteen minutes. We bared our hearts to each other—our disappointments and our failures. In truth, cancer had caught our marriage at a low point. We had been running on empty for a while, and if God was to move this mountain of cancer, we had a lot of unforgiveness to move out of the way. This high-octane cleansing was based on what I knew of Mark 11:22–26.

In Christian circles, Mark 11:22–26 is often referenced in terms of healing. It's a power packed verse that has always intimidated me. However, what the Holy Spirit brought to my attention years ago was contained in those verses.

And Jesus answered saying to them, "*Have faith in God.* Truly I say to you, whoever says to this mountain, 'Be taken up and cast into the sea,' and does not doubt in his heart, but believes that what he says is going to happen, it will be granted him. Therefore I say to you, all things for which you pray and ask, believe that you have received them, and they will be granted you. *Whenever you stand praying, forgive, if you have anything against anyone, so that your Father who is in heaven will also forgive you your transgressions. But if you do not forgive, neither will your Father who is in heaven forgive your transgressions.*"

There is a lot in this Scripture, isn't there? Don't doubt in your heart, ask and believe, give forgiveness or you won't be forgiven. How in our humanness is any mountain, illness, or anything else, ever moved then?

Jesus tells us to return to the innocence of a child. Have you ever witnessed a child's faith? They are so pure and believing. They don't have theological discussions and they don't look to other worldly examples, but they just dance in the possibilities of God. Gary and I use the image of a trusting child as we approach our relationship with God. We take Him at His Word and try to keep things really simple.

Jesus said we are to have faith in God. We are not to have faith in our ability to love God, not faith in our works, not faith in anything but God. But here is the catch: if you are not looking at healing through the faith of a child, your adulthood will run wild as it desperately tries to "do" faith as a means of proving you have enough of it. When Christians qualify faith as an action, they are looking at themselves as the measurement of faithfulness. "Do I love God enough? Did I pray enough? Did I read enough Scripture? Did I serve enough?" Reading Scripture, praying, and advancing the kingdom through service are all definitely faith builders because they reinforce God's nature in our inmost being. However, for Gary and me, faith in God was a simple act of vulnerable, obedient, surrender: "Yes, Lord, You are the great I AM. We trust You to be God in our life. Please take our lives and do what You will. Lead us, heal us, discipline us, grow us, forgive us, and yes, lavishly bless us, not because we are worthy but because You are God."

In verse 23 Jesus says we are not to doubt. I fail before I finish reading the verse. What about all those prayers that go unanswered? How about all the suffering, poverty, and loneliness that people experience all over the world? Of course we doubt. We are human, hardwired to doubt, reason, and question. However, one of the most wonderful things about God is that He knows us so well that He has designed a contingency plan for where we fall short. It's called repentance, and His Son paid the ultimate price so that we have it as an option.

Let's clear up the area of where we doubt. This verse says that we are not to doubt in our heart. It doesn't say we are not to doubt in our mind but in our heart. Have you ever thought the two are separate? I doubt in my mind all the time. I have thousands of questions for God that are irrelevant if I understood Him completely. The truth is that I will never understand Him completely this side of heaven. We just don't have that capacity. Thankfully, His nature is patient and forgiving, and He works with us as we are able to understand. However, my heart—now that is steadfast on Him, a completely different entity altogether. In my heart I know He is a God capable of the miraculous, and my mind, well, that is coming into greater agreement every day.

Before you stop reading, I am not saying it's good to doubt in your mind, and as you read further you will see the trouble it caused me. However, if you find yourself spending time in doubt, God's contingency plan of repentance is built to deal with your thoughts as well as your actions, especially while He is in the process of purifying who you are in Him—mind, body, and spirit.

Let me be very clear here: it is a dangerous business to sit in doubt for too long, especially if you are not countering the doubt of your mind with food for your heart, such as reading Scripture. Why is this dangerous? Because when you are praying to move a mountain, doubt depletes your faith. It gets your eyes off the nature of God and onto the physical realities of this world. God works above and beyond physical realities. They do not hold Him or contain Him. So if you find yourself entertaining doubt, the answer is sweet and simple: repent and get your eyes back on God's nature.

The beauty of His plan for our humanness is in its simplicity. Jesus took on our sin when He died on the cross. All we have to do is believe it has been done and bring our sinful nature back to Him for forgiveness. He actually loves it when we repent, when we confess our sins to Him and ask for His forgiveness. Doing so means we are in a trusting relationship with Him, and His Son didn't die in vain.

Jesus said, "Therefore I say to you, all things for which you pray and ask, believe that you have received them, and they will be granted you" (Mark 11:24). There is so much unsaid in this verse. It's an amazing exercise in trust, yet the word *trust* isn't mentioned anywhere. Pray. Ask. Believe. Receive. Really, is it that easy? Hardly! Our human nature is always in the way, and so are our circumstances. Otherwise, Scripture wouldn't refer to them as "mountains."

In 1 Chronicles 5:20, Scripture says that the armies of Reuben, Gad, and Manasseh were helped in battle because "they cried out to God in the battle, and He answered their prayers because they trusted in Him." Moving mountains in your life is definitely worthy of the term "battle." Trust, for Gary and me, was something that needed to be reinforced daily through God's signs and wonders, the kindness and prayers of Team Brausen, the reading and quoting of Scripture, our own prayers, and simply resting in God's omnipotence.

We had to stand, trust, and believe in God's nature and promises before we received medical proof that Gary was cured. We weren't always successful in this area. I hate to beat this thing silly, but as soon as we were less than believing, we simply repented. In between the initial prayer and victory was surgery, second opinions, chemotherapy, radiation, and then a two-year waiting period.[1]

Verses 25–26 are why I was insistent in getting Gary out of bed that morning. They spoke to my heart and the state of our

---

1   If you know Scripture well, you might be thinking Reuben, Gad, and Manasseh were powerfully trained warriors, and they would have won without trusting in God. But have not many wonderfully trained warriors fallen to lesser foes? Think of Gideon, or David and Goliath. Even the most prepared warrior's are not prepared enough without keeping their eyes on God.

marriage. Gary and I had let a whole lot of nothing build up over the years, and how was Gary going to be able to lean on me if old junk kept getting in the way? How could I pray for him earnestly if secretly I was still angry about past mistakes? In turn, how in the world could we approach our wonderful Father in heaven and ask for mercy when we couldn't give mercy to each other?

By Saturday mid-afternoon, the Duluth wind had really picked up and the temperature dropped rapidly. We had stopped in Two Harbors and the boys wanted to run the length of a peninsula that jetted far out into the lake. I took the boys out and Gary stayed back in the car because it was way too cold for him to be outside, plus he was feeling simply rotten.

Bennett, Alec, and I had made it all the way to the end of the peninsula, had turned around, and were making our way back. We were the only ones crazy enough to be out in that weather—it was freezing. I was surprised to see a man walking toward us. As we continued to walk back toward the car, the gentlemen's shape came into clearer focus. It was Gary. My eyes welled up and I ran toward him. "What are you doing out here?" I shouted over the wind.

"I'm not going to sit back and watch you and the kids do things without me!" he shouted back. "I just can't sit back and let cancer take my life away." I know it was super cheesy, though at the time it didn't feel cheesy: I felt like my man, with God's help, was going to give cancer one heck of a fight.

Three Weeks Feels Like a Lifetime

For by these He has granted to us His precious and magnificent promises, so that by them you may become partakers of the divine nature, having escaped the corruption that is in the world by lust (2 Peter 1:4).

The following week was a blur of doctor's appointments. We were assigned a nurse coordinator who would assist us through the whole process. Her name was Jody. In those early days, I felt sorry for Jody. She was the front man (or, I guess, the front woman), the organizer. She was honest and forthright in how much information she could share with us. In fact, she would often say to Gary as he pressed her for more information, "That is something your oncologist, Dr. Leach, will answer for you."

Gary was understandably tenacious in his need for information. He asked her question after question, trying to eek out any morsel of hope that he could. She would no more dodge one question that he would ask another. You can't blame him. Waiting through the process of testing is one of the hardest parts of the cancer journey to be taken.

Immediately after Gary's diagnosis, he was scheduled for another CT scan. When the results were in, Jody called Gary to set up our first oncology appointment. Gary caught her completely off guard by the way he asked questions.

"Gary, your CT scan results are in," she said over the phone. "I would like to schedule your appointment with Dr. Leach—he is a great oncologist."

"Jody, can you explain again what they are looking for on the CT scan?" Gary asked.

"Sure, we are looking to see if the cancer is contained to your lung or if it has moved to other places in your body. We are also looking to see how aggressive your cancer is behaving."

"How do you know that again?" Gary asked.

"Well, the CT scan lights up metastasized cancer. So your oncologist can tell where the cancer is and how aggressive it is behaving."

"Has it stayed within my lungs?"

(*Smooth Gary*, I thought as I was sitting beside him.)

"Yes," she said.

(At this point, I knew she was done. Gary was going in for the kill.)

Gary fell to the floor in gratitude. "Thank You, Lord! Thank You, Lord!" he sobbed. He gained his composure and then asked, "Well, if you know that, you must also be able to see how aggressive the cancer is behaving. Is it very aggressive?" Gary pressed.

Jody paused a moment. "Gary, this is information for your oncologist to share," replied Jody.

"But you can see my scan. Is it aggressive? You have to tell me. I can't wait for another three days. Jody, please…"

(Nicely played, my dear husband. Desperate pleading. Could you blame him?)

"It doesn't appear to be very aggressive," was her reply. But then she said, "But, Gary, you need to talk to your oncologist."

In Jody's defense, Hitler would have fallen to Gary's pleas for information. They were so heartfelt and he was so desperate. Her response gave him peace for the next seventy-two hours, something we desperately needed during that time. Cancer had brought with it an ally, an equally devious tyrant, the spirit of anxiety. We were battling on two fronts now—the fight in his body and now a battle for his mind.

OUR FIRST ONCOLOGY APPOINTMENT: THE BOMB DROPS

The morning of our first oncology appointment was full of anticipation. We dropped the boys off at school, then in relative silence we drove into the city. As Gary parked the car, we sat for just a moment. There wasn't much to say.

Walking into the lobby of Minnesota Oncology felt like the first day at a new school. We noticed the smell of coffee, a sign that read PLEASE WAIT HERE FOR THE NEXT AVAILABLE RECEPTIONIST, and the calming color scheme—overall, it was a very positive environment. We also noticed a packed lobby. There were tons of people, and many of them were looking at the "newbies"—us.

I now know what they were thinking. "I wonder which one is sick? Him or her?" "Boy, they're young." "I wonder how they are doing?" We know this because as we became pros at cancer, these were the thoughts that crossed our mind too when someone new came in. The look of the newbies is obvious. It's like they entered a black hole and have come into a new universe. It is a place that no one ever expects to find him- or herself.

Jody was correct that the CT scan did show the cancer to be about a three out of ten on the aggressive scale, but the biopsy was showing something else. The cancer was cloaking itself, fooling Gary's body into not paying it any attention, as it very aggressively made its way through his left lung. They considered the cancer to be in the Bronchoalveolar family, but it wasn't behaving typically—so that category really didn't fit.

Our meeting with Dr. Leach was heartbreaking, to say the least—he didn't pull any punches. We were in a fight for Gary's life. Dr. Leach would need to order more tests. There were genetic markers that could be helpful in fighting this cancer—they needed to see if it had spread into his lymphatic wall, into his bones, or even into his brain. And there would definitely be chemotherapy involved. Dr. Leach balanced this information with many stories of hope, but his parting words hit us in the stomach: "You will want to get your affairs in order."

We went into the lobby to wait for Brynn, Dr. Leach's oncology nurse, with the look of a deer in the headlights. I honestly don't remember much after that. And I was too numb to pray.

CONVERSATIONS NO ONE WANTS TO HAVE

After meeting with Dr. Leach, Gary and I needed time to process all that was going on. But that time was quickly becoming a scarce commodity. We left the oncology office and went for a walk around Normandale Lake.

Two years earlier we had lost our dear neighbor Barb to leukemia. Barb's struggle was torturous for her and her family. She was basically hospitalized from her diagnosis on Mother's Day of 2009 to her home hospice care in December of the same year. On one of her brief homestays during that six-month period, she met me in the front yard. She looked me squarely in the eye and said that if she had known the pain and suffering she would need to go through just to die anyway, she would have made a different choice. I know Barb to be a fierce fighter, so I took her comment to be a measurement of the amount of suffering she had endured over the past few months.

Now that we were facing a similar scenario, Barb's words echoed in my mind. As much as I didn't want to face this option, I was going to have to bring up the topic of treatment with Gary. As I was trying to work up the courage to broach the subject, I couldn't look at him. The more I tried to be strong, the more I trembled inside.

"Gary, your treatment could be brutal," I finally said. "I can't ask you to go through that kind of suffering for my sake or the boys'. This has to be your choice and I will support any decision you make." I didn't believe a word I said because inside my head I was screaming, "Fight for us! Please, fight for us!"

Gary didn't say a word. I stopped walking and looked at him. "What are you thinking?" I finally asked.

"There is not one doubt in mind that I will do anything

it takes to fight," he replied. "I'm scared to death, but I'm still planning on growing old with you, and my boys still need their dad. Rosey, I just have to win this fight."

Relief washed over me as we stood on the path and hugged for a long time. To everyone who walked past us that afternoon we probably looked just like any other couple enjoying a little springtime PDA.

When we got home, I called my big sister Terri and completely broke down. I am blessed with nine amazing siblings, and with each sibling I have a special relationship that I cherish. Terri is ten years older than me, and our bond goes back to when she used to carry me into her bed when I was a baby. There are many stories of how I loved to snuggle as close as possible to her—so close, in fact, that she would often wake up soaking wet from my leaking cloth diaper. She has always been my "big" sister, and I needed her right then and there. I don't even remember our conversation except that I cried a lot.

Gary went into work to talk to Kevin, his boss. Dr. Leach had indicated that we would need everything Gary had to beat this cancer; working through treatment was not going to be an option. This was going to be a hard conversation for Gary to have.

Gary was hired by Seagate Technology in 1996 as an engineering manager. He loved Seagate for all the reasons you would expect: it challenged him, there was always something new being created, and the pulse was invigorating. Telling his boss that he needed to step down filled him with dread. He was worried that technology would pass him by, that once he recovered he would have nothing to contribute. What Gary didn't know was that as soon as he was diagnosed with cancer, Kevin had called me. We had been in communication for the better part of the previous ten days.

Gary stood in Kevin's doorway. "Kevin, I won't be able to work while I'm being treated."

"Gary, I have already spoken to Rosey. I understand what you are up against. You need to fight this thing with everything you have got."

"I will be back," Gary said to him. "I just don't know when, but I will be better than I am now."

"I know you will, and when you are ready there will be a job for you," Kevin reassured him.

Before Gary left the building, he needed to meet with his colleague Chris. Chris had lost his teenage son a few years prior, and Gary knew him to be an amazing man of faith. They discussed many things, but what Gary was seeking was someone who understood how to bear life-and-death circumstances and still stand in faith. Gary went to Chris's whiteboard and drew a picture of a cup.

"Chris, what I have to do is concentrate on the portion of the cup that is full and keep my eyes on the Lord," Gary said. "I have a feeling it's not going to be as simple as that though." Thankfully, he had no idea of how right he was.

MIND GAMES AND GOD'S PROMISES

Anxiety. Worry. Fear. Their sole job is to destroy the gift of peace that our Lord and Savior has given to us. Jesus said, "Peace I leave with you; My peace I give to you; not as the world gives do I give to you. Do not let your heart be troubled, nor let it be fearful" (John 14:27). Anxiety, worry, and fear try to steal this peace. It's a direct assault on Jesus's precious gift that is given to us in Him. They are thieves of the highest order, and they were going after Gary and my boys.

Once Gary was in the recovery phase of his journey, he was able to link his anxiety to what he had witnessed as a young teenager. In a short period of time, Gary had lost both his twenty-nine-year-old uncle Tom and his dear grandma Maeble to cancer. Watching these two people suffer filled Gary with certain dread. In those days, there wasn't a whole lot of attention paid to processing your feelings, nor were the cancer treatments of today available. At a very impressionable age, Gary watched their suffering, personalized it, and stuffed it deep inside.

He was later able to tell me that being diagnosed with cancer was his single greatest fear. However, at the time of his diagnosis, these personal revelations were still a few years away. All I knew at this point was that we were in the throes of a battle; thankfully, God never leaves His beloved without weapons.

In Ephesians 6:10–17, Paul tells us to put on the whole armor of God so that we can stand against the attacks of the enemy. He writes:

> Finally, be strong in the Lord and in the strength of His might. Put on the full armor of God, so that you will be able to stand firm against the schemes of the devil. For our struggle is not against flesh and blood, but against the rulers, against the powers, against the world forces

of this darkness, against the spiritual forces of wickedness in the heavenly places. Therefore, take up the full armor of God, so that you will be able to resist in the evil day, and having done everything, to stand firm. Stand firm therefore, having girded your loins with truth, and having put on the breastplate of righteousness, and having shod your feet with the preparation of the gospel of peace; in addition to all, taking up the shield of faith with which you will be able to extinguish all the flaming arrows of the evil one. And take the helmet of salvation, and the sword of the Spirit, which is the word of God.

Putting on the armor of God makes you feel strong, doesn't it? I love to envision myself like a warrior when I prayerfully put on the armor of God. Did you notice that there are only three pieces of armor that take our cooperation at some level? The helmet of salvation, which is the mind of Christ where we choose to conform our thoughts in obedience, the shield of faith, and the sword of the Spirit are active pieces of armor that we must choose to pick up, hold firm, and wield. Everything else God has done for us through the death and resurrection of His Son, Jesus.

Helmet of Salvation

In 2 Corinthians 10:4–5, Paul tells us that though we walk in the flesh we do not war in the flesh; rather, we must take every thought captive to the obedience of Christ.

Think of how many times you have heard in your head

derogatory comments about yourself, things such as "You won't succeed," "You're different," and "No one understands," etc. These are thoughts of the enemy, not thoughts of God. God loves you. He created you. He knit you together in your mother's womb with love and purpose. He would never, and I mean *never*, discourage you or bring you down in any way. It's not His nature.

Taking every thought captive to the obedience of Christ means we grab hold of our thoughts and battle against the negative, detracting, unpure thoughts that come into our minds. Yes, it's very difficult to do in actuality. It's a real battle, but it can be won by simply keeping our eyes fixed on the Lord. For Gary and me, this took a lot of discipline and forming a plan on how to implement this on a daily basis.

This fight took on different forms for each member of my family at different times throughout the journey. Gary was plagued with anxiety and worry. And who can blame him? I battled the mental exhaustion of standing in truth, and the boys wrestled with sideways fears that bubbled up out of nowhere, having nothing and everything to do with cancer.

We prayed, we quoted Scripture, we affirmed each other, we used distraction, and we confessed our doubts and our weaknesses. At one point Gary counted quoting Scripture out loud over twenty-five times in the period of an hour. We desperately needed to do everything we could to stand our ground in our minds, because that is often the battlefield that is attacked first.[2]

---

2   If this is striking a cord in your spirit, you may want to read *The Battlefield of the Mind* by Joyce Meyer. It will be a worthwhile investment of your time.

Shield of Faith

Faith. The Bible has a lot to say about it. Jesus refers to having "enough" faith at least ten different times, so you know it is vitally important to our lives here on earth. The question most of us grapple with is, faith in what? Faith that there is a God? Faith that you have served Him well? Or is it faith in a higher plan? The truth is that I have yet to meet a human who hasn't struggled with "enough" faith in the face of seemingly insurmountable challenges at some point in their life.

Gary and I were no different. A quick inventory of our lives showed that we were lacking on all fronts. The only tangible faith we could measure was that we both were steadfast in our belief that God is God. He has made promises and covenants with us that He will not break. We trust and have faith in His character, not our own.

Psalm 91:4 also brought us clarity during this time: "He will cover you with His pinions, and under His wings you may seek refuge; His faithfulness is a shield and bulwark." We took this to mean that His faithfulness, not our own, would help build our faith. He is so good at being God.

Sword of the Spirit

The Bible is full of information about the importance of speaking out the Word of God over all our situations. My favorite view from theologians much more studied than me is that speaking out the Word of God bubbles up from our belief in God. Belief that God spoke this whole world into being, belief that He who is capable of hanging the moon in the sky, turning on the stars, controlling the tide, as well as making the artichoke, is also capable of breathing His Word into life.

Understandably, this can be hard to grasp at times. Of course, God has a perfect example for us in His Son. Satan confronted Jesus after being in the desert for forty days without food. What weapon did He use to defeat the temptations of the enemy? Yep, it was Scripture. Nothing fancy; there were no lightning bolts. It was just plain Scripture. And what did Satan do as Jesus quoted Scripture? He fled. He fled because he knows Scripture is God-breathed truth, and he can't stand to be around it being spoken out loud.

Over the years the impact of quoting Scripture out loud has been lost. For most of us, if we have ever memorized Scripture, it was when we were kids. And in times of difficulty, most of us are not aware of the power of the Word and how it can heal us, bring life to our hearts, creating hope deep within us.

Our problem was that Gary was so new to the Lord that he didn't have much Scripture memorized. And, in truth, neither did I. Thankfully, years earlier a book was given to me called *God's Promises for Your Every Need*. In this book, Gary could look up any emotion he was feeling and repeat Scripture out loud over himself related to that specific emotion. Depressed? There is Scripture for you. Confused? There is Scripture for that too. Under the subject of healing, guess what we found? Jeremiah 30:17—the very Scripture God had given me that night in Duluth.

As the days wore on, anxiety was gaining a foothold in our lives. Gary would change his shirt several times a day, he followed me from room to room, and he couldn't sit still. Antsy doesn't even begin to describe his constant movement. He had a terrible time focusing, and the only thing that would give him rest was the *God's Promises* book. Ever an engineer, he stuck to a precise plan. Anxiety equaled quoting Scripture—no relenting. We said Scripture like it was prescribed medicine. In our case, this was all day long. It is the only thing that gave him any peace.

While anxiety attacked his mind, cancer was punishing in his system. Is it because he finally knew what was draining his energy that he felt exponentially worse? Sleep was essentially nonexistent during this time. Coughing fits claimed the whole night. We waited for more test results, genetic markers, and held onto hope.

Lack of sleep was also impeding my ability to be a caregiver and mom. Completely divided between my husband and my children, what brought me the most comfort were the words my dad and mom had given me when we told them of Gary's diagnosis. My dad told me, "Rosey, God's grace is sufficient. Somehow, God gives you the ability to bear the trial you are in. He will be faithful to give you what you need." Mom and Dad were speaking from experience. They had survived my dad's near-death experience with MS and the years of recovery it took before he could return to a normal life.

During those early nights, I would prop myself up on the end of the couch, Gary would lean on me, and I could wrap my arms around him. This position was the only way he had peace in his mind and his coughing would be somewhat controlled. These were sleepless nights, but as I comforted Gary

I felt God wrapping His wings around us both. Meditating on God's presence brought me an unexplainable rest. I was exhausted but somehow had enough energy for everything the next day would bring.

No one wants to be a cardholder in "God's grace is sufficient" club. But when you are facing seemingly insurmountable challenges, it's the sweetest refreshment to be confident in a God who promises to walk with you through all circumstances—it's rest in and of itself. If you leave with nothing from our story except this one truth, Gary and I will be elated.

Finally, Gary agreed to try a sleep aid with an antianxiety booster. It was like receiving a pony for Christmas. Since he was sleeping better, he was feeling better. We got our head above the water and started to formulate a plan. Pray, confess Scripture out loud, and stand on God's promises. Then repeat.

Chapter 4

Our CaringBridge

You also joining in helping us through your prayers, so that thanks may be given by many persons on our behalf for the favor bestowed on us through the prayers of many (2 Corinthians 1:11).

One of my favorite healing Scriptures is when Jesus healed the paralyzed man who was lowered down through the roof by his friends. Mark recounts the story for us:

When [Jesus] had come back to Capernaum several days afterward, it was heard that He was at home. And many were gathered together, so that there was no longer room, not even near the door; and He was speaking the word to them. And they came, bringing to Him a paralytic, carried by four men. Being unable to get to Him because of the crowd, they removed the roof above Him; and when they had dug an opening, they let down the pallet on which the paralytic was lying. And Jesus seeing their faith said to the paralytic, "Son, your sins are forgiven" (Mark 2:1–5).

Don't you love this story? The paralyzed man's friends gather him up, scramble through the crowds, break through the roof of the house in which Jesus was teaching, and lower their friend down into the very presence of Jesus. I know Jesus must have been smiling ear to ear as he saw the faith of this man's four friends.

Our friends and family didn't break down a physical roof on Gary's behalf, but with their prayers they raised it all the way to heaven, past the pearly gates, and right into God's throne room. They brought Gary right to the feet of Jesus by their prayers.

Almost immediately after we had met with Mark and Pat, I made a decision against Gary's will. He was really not on board, and I mean *really*. I asked my friend Heidi to open up a CaringBridge website for us. CaringBridge is a site where families facing difficult medical situations can keep in contact with friends and family. It is also a place where friends and family can leave notes and affirmations for the person who is sick.

I understood his resistance to the idea—only people with huge problems have a CaringBridge site. Well, yes, and we were now part of "those" people. Plus, Gary is considerably more private than I am. So, as you can imagine, this was really beyond comfortable for him. It is embarrassing to admit, but Gary has more than a few hysterical stories of when I have gone against his wishes in the past—humdinger stories that the *Lucille Ball Show* would have loved to use; however, setting up the CaringBridge site is not one of them.

I believed this was a time for communication, authenticity, and prayer. As hindsight would have it, the reasons for Gary's hesitation and my own insensitivity to his position came into clear focus. But what's a strong-willed Irish girl to do when her man is in serious need of help? Here is our opening story on the CaringBridge site:

> Before we begin, please know that Gary and I stand in our faith that curing the cancer is God's job and our job is to remind Satan that he has lost this battle. Your prayers help us finish this race strong. It is our belief that no matter what statistics say, God has the last word…and He is really good at what He does.
>
> We will update the journal as often as we can, so visit often to read the latest journal entries, visit the photo gallery, and write us a note in our guestbook.

We never got to those photos for the gallery, but we were faithful to keep the journal updated. Our friends and family were amazingly faithful to leave us prayers, Scripture passages, jokes, and songs. They shopped for us, entertained the kids, made meals, visited, weeded and planted our garden, shoveled our driveway, had our windows cleaned, and never stopped filling us with hope. Their CaringBridge entries and all their acts of kindness became our lifeline during this time. On hundreds of occasions throughout our journey, I would read Gary and the boys guestbook entries, and each time we as a family came away stronger. How could we be so blessed?

How could we be so loved?

Somewhere during those first three weeks, our dear friend and former neighbor Barb Blake made a hockey analogy about Gary's battle on CaringBridge. It stuck, and Team Brausen was born. Anyone reading our site became a member of Team Brausen, and Gary was the captain. This fight was going to have three periods: diagnosis, fight, and victory! It was perfect for my hockey-playing husband. It helped him not feel so defeated in the process, and it helped our whole family fight in so many intangible ways. We were all benefactors from Team Brausen. Here is an excerpt from one of our CaringBridge entries that depicts the power of prayer.

> I have not written much about the boys on this site, basically because I am a human "she bear." However, I think this little story is an exception because I know many of you are praying specifically for their protection against fear, anxiety, and worry.
>
> Last night as I was saying goodnight to Bennett, I approached the subject of the cancer and asked him if he was scared for Dad this week. He responded, "I am not scared, Mom. Is it OK that I am not scared?"
>
> "Well, that depends, Bennett, on why you are not scared. Why do you think you are not scared?"
>
> "I don't know. I just completely trust God that He is taking care of Dad, no matter what. I can't explain it, but I just have a peace in my heart whenever I think of this week. This doesn't mean I haven't been angry or scared at all. It just means that I haven't been scared lately."

"Bennett, do you know what it means to be cloaked in prayer? It is what you are experiencing right now. People have been praying for you 24/7 for almost three weeks. They have been praying that the peace that transcends all understanding will be your constant companion."

"That's Jesus, right?" he asked. "Cool."

"Yeah, cool."

Alec's response has been easier to read right now as he has taken to helping Gary count the days until surgery. "Don't worry, Dad, only four more days until they just cut that cancer right out of you!"

Every member of Team Brausen, every act of kindness, and every prayer lifted changed the course of Gary's illness. From Cheryl Higgins's (my prayer partner) pleas before the Lord, to Shirley's (Gary's mom) persistence to get Gary on every prayer list possible, Team Brausen made it known to anyone and everyone that Gary needed prayer.

As time passed, we learned that Team Brausen was not just for Gary, but others were finding a certain solace in guestbook entries as well. What also came to our attention is that there is a huge void in help and support for other illnesses, such as mental illness, depression, or addictions. Those suffering from such illnesses and their caregivers could also use the support of a Team Brausen, but their struggles were cloaked in secrecy, embarrassment, or a lack of understanding. It is my prayer that one day all those who are suffering from any sort of illness will feel free to have a blog or a CaringBridge site.

PROMISE OF THE DAY

In those early days, another monumental event took place. Our dear friend Julie took to praying Scripture for us every morning. Julie is an amazing woman of God, full of grace, honesty, humor, discipline, and encouragement. Early on, when I would tell her about the anxiety Gary was facing, she would send Scriptures to us via e-mail so we could take them with us throughout the day. She titled the Scriptures "Promises of the Day."

Four years later, she is still e-mailing them to us every morning. But now she sends them to family and friends all around the world too. Through our journey, the Lord birthed a prayer intercessor and a new ministry that is bringing encouragement to many people. It is an unexpected silver lining in our journey that still brings me an unexplainable joy.

CaringBridge and Julie's "Promises of the Day" became our heartbeat as Gary's situation came into clearer focus. It was two weeks since a diagnosis and we now had a medical team put together for Gary. Our team consisted of an oncologist, pathologist, pulmonologist, thoracic surgeon, radiology oncologist, and our oncology nurse. We met again with Dr. Leach, which was a very interesting appointment, to say the least.

The week before I could have walked past Dr. Leach and perhaps only smiled in passing, but the week we met with him again I was shaking his hand and praying that he was paying attention during medical school, and that God had given him an extra measure of wisdom as it pertained to this cancer.

Gary asked him this question, "If there was a line in front of you, where a conservative approach to cancer was positioned at one end and an aggressive approach to cancer on the other, where would you put yourself?"

Dr. Leach got real close to Gary, and looked him straight in the eye, then said, "I'm very aggressive—no question—very aggressive." We loved that man.

Gary did not test positive for any genetic markers, which would have allowed for more targeted and optimal therapy after surgery. This was disappointing news, but it was balanced with a clear brain MRI, PET scan, and bone scan. Now we knew that cancer had not migrated out of Gary's lung into other parts of his body.

Waiting for these test results filled us with dread. There was no amount of distraction that could take away the feeling of sickness in our stomachs, though we tried mightily. It was difficult to rest in the Lord, it took a lot to stand, and we learned the truth that "waiting" is an active verb. The stakes were indeed high. If they could get his lung out, then we might have a chance. If cancer had spread outside the lung, however, then his odds of beating this cancer were drastically different.

The last and final test was to ensure that the cancer was nowhere to be found in the space between the lungs with a surgical procedure called a mediastinoscopy. In this procedure, the lymph nodes and tissue were sampled and biopsied to make sure no cancer was present. Thoracic surgeon Matt Graczyk would conduct this procedure and the lung retraction if the lymph nodes were clear.

Dr. Graczyk was the ideal surgeon and perfect fit for Gary and our most difficult case. From the first meeting with him, Gary and I liked him instantly. He was approachable, real, someone you feel like you would have over to your house for dinner. He actually reminds me a lot of my little brother Paul so much that I often just wanted to hug him. He is that relatable.

Gary was quickly becoming known by our medical team for his pressing questions. His first meeting with Dr. Graczyk was no different. After Dr. Graczyk gave Gary a brief synopsis of his situation, Gary looked directly into his eyes and asked, "This is kind of a big deal for me; you're going to be taking out my left lung. Are you any good?"

Dr. Graczyk didn't miss a beat. "Yes, very," he said with a big grin across his face. This was the kind of confidence that made us feel comfortable, but before the lung retraction could even take place we still needed an all clear from the mediastinoscopy. "Please, Lord, let those lymph nodes be clear!"

The mediastinoscopy procedure was scheduled for Monday, April 4. Gary and I spent the weekend prior getting ready physically, emotionally, and spiritually. We were all ready to go, but on Sunday night we learned Dr. Graczyk was detained in Colorado due to heavy snowfall and we would have to wait until Tuesday before the procedure could occur. This doesn't sound so bad, does it? Just a one-day delay, but it was devastating. Gary and I were as ready as we could be, and this delay reminded us that we were not in control of much in our lives.

On Tuesday the procedure was conducted as scheduled.

Seeing Dr. Graczyk after the mediastinoscopy is still one of my favorite memories of this entire journey. Gary's dad had kept me company while Gary was in surgery. We had left the waiting room to get some fresh air, and as we were returning we could see a man in scrubs coming out of the waiting room.

"Rosey! Rosey!" he yelled as he practically skipped toward us (it wasn't really a skip but a very happy kind of walk). "There was no cancer in the lymph nodes. Rosey, I really dug around and there was no cancer!"

Finally, a break. I don't know how I responded, but today I still chuckle at his unrepressed joy—very un-Hollywood-surgeon-like, but boy did it fill our tanks. "Rosey, we are going to get that lung out. It's the break we have been looking for!" he continued. "Get in there and see Gary. This is great news!"

Now Heni and I were the ones who were happy walking into the recovery room. This was great news indeed. We would have to wait for another day for the official pathology report, but at that moment we were ecstatic. Here was our CaringBridge entry the day the pathology report came in:

Pathology returned an all clear in Gary's lymph nodes. Surgery is on for tomorrow morning. Sleep peacefully, Team Brausen. Your prayers have been heard.

The next morning my healthy, athletic, nonsmoking husband was being prepped for surgery to remove his left lung. Odd for my very inclusive personality type, but I did not want anyone with me in the waiting room. To this day I still don't understand why, but I just didn't. All I can remember is that

I was craving quiet. I wanted to pray. I wanted to hold my breath; I wanted to read *People* magazine and escape.

Thankfully, Gary's family would have none of it, and Gary's dad, Heni, his mom, Shirley, and younger brother, Chris, and I all wished Gary well as he went into surgery. Gary was rolled back into the operating room with his *God's Promises* book in hand.

GOD'S SENSE OF HUMOR

As we were waiting for Gary to be brought up from surgery, Jody had stopped by to see how we were doing. She also wanted to tell us about another cancer patient who, two days earlier, had also had his lung removed. This particular gentleman had been a smoker with a heart condition and not in the best of health, but he was doing fabulous after surgery. If it all worked out, she thought it would be a good idea if we met him.

Jody left and we waited for a few more minutes before a patient walked in and sat down at the computer in the waiting room. I will never forget my first impression of Kurt—he had a joyful little step and was very friendly. He greeted each and every one of us and then proceeded to work on the computer.

Gary's family and I started to discuss what Jody had told us and how encouraging it was to have someone doing so well on the same floor. We even pondered if Gary and this gentleman could perhaps help each other through recovery. The patient at the computer turned to us, apologized for eavesdropping, and introduced himself as Kurt Anderson, the very man who also lost a lung just two days prior.

I can't tell you how shocked I was that this was the man Jody was just telling us about. He was so friendly, in no pain, looked fantastic, and was completely looped up on really good pain meds. We still laugh about this today.

What we didn't know then but understand now is God's sense of humor and perfect plan. The chances of surviving lung cancer are about 16 percent; it was even less for Kurt and Gary. We were soon to learn that Gary's cancer was extremely aggressive and Kurt's body was not in a great position to survive what he was going to have to endure.

Gary lost his left lung and Kurt his right. Gary is a six-foot-one-inch nonsmoking athlete; Kurt is a five-foot-seven-inch former smoker. They are the most unusual pair. But between the two of them, they cover the whole male spectrum of lung cancer. They are great friends and make a dynamic duo speaking team. Only God can plan something so perfect.

Kurt Anderson

Chapter 5

The Fight Begins

The official beginning of Gary's recovery started the first evening in the hospital after his surgery. Still loopy from the pain medication, the anesthetic, and the shock of a very radical procedure, Gary insisted on standing on his own. Surrounded by a team of doctors who attempted to convince him that this was not necessary, he stood on his own two feet with tubes and wires coming from all parts of his body. The next day, he even took his first steps and was later visited by Dr. Graczyk who stopped in to see Gary and check on his handiwork.

"Congratulations, Gary," Dr. Graczyk said, "you have just survived the most painful surgery known to man."

"I hope I get a kick*** trophy," Gary said. "I got up and walked already."

"That's great! Your athleticism will assist in helping you get well. Keep at it but don't push too hard."

I sat there and listened to this male banter go back and forth for some time. My first thought was, "If you know my husband, you would chain him to his bed, because of course he will push it too hard." My second thought was to thank God for sending people into our lives at the perfect time to bring normalcy, camaraderie, and humor when we needed it the most.

Gary was doing so well right after surgery that we let our guard down. "This wasn't that bad," I thought to myself. But then evening fell and all the wheels fell off with it. Gary started to spike a fever, he had uncontrollable pain in his neck and shoulder, and he was having a reaction to the pain medication.

The staff was doing everything they possibly could to make him comfortable, but nothing seemed to be working. Throughout the process I noticed a particularly kind and peaceful orderly who would come into the room, watch the chaos, bring water, and fluff Gary's pillows. On one of his trips in to see Gary, he brought me some hospital slippers. I looked at him quite surprised. "For me?" I asked.

"Yes, you take," he said. "It all helps, and this night is difficult."

I had been a rock. No tears, no fretting, holding Gary's hand, comforting him, calling the kids, and working with the nurses. But this one simple gesture broke me to pieces. My eyes welled up, I thanked him, and he bowed as he left the room, never to be seen again. Why are the simplest acts of kindness so disarming?

Right before dawn the fever came down, they found a pain medication that worked, and Gary finally slept. For the longest time I sat there and just watched him. I didn't pray, I didn't cry, I didn't think of Bennett and Alec—I was completely numb. I slipped into sleep with not one thought in my head.

Day two and three brought the return of my loving husband. Gary kept asking the nursing staff for benchmarks just so he could know how to beat them. When they said walking once around the floor would be good, he walked twice. When they gave him a goal to walk at least six laps around the hospital floor the following morning, the new shift nurse was at a disadvantage, not knowing he had walked six laps the day before. Smiling, Gary said, "I think I'll do ten instead." She was amazed. And he looked proud.

You know the old saying, "No pain, no gain"? Well, Gary began to experience a little pain for his gain after that, which was frustrating to be sure. His schedule was pretty set—eat, walk, and sleep. They took him off the epidural the following day, thus regulating the pain with oral medication. He wasn't sure about visitors yet, because each day was bringing something new, and his focus on getting well was making him extremely tired.

It had been a few good days all around. Gary even agreed to have the boys stop by for a visit. Up to this point, he was reluctant to have them see him in pain. I am still so grateful for how my family stepped in to keep the boys entertained while Gary was in the hospital. This was indeed no easy task, so the entertainment was of much higher quality than usual. I remember thinking Bennett and Alec are going to look back on this time of their life and think cancer wasn't so bad—they got to go to Timberwolves games, the zoo, movies, out to eat at restaurants of their choice, and on and on.

When my younger brother Paul brought the boys to the hospital, I could read all over his face that though they were fully entertained, their veneer was beginning to crack. Bennett was becoming an expert at stuffing his feelings, smiling, and saying everything was fine. Alec was pensive and preoccupied with his teeth and a host of other anxieties and fears.

They were both extremely relieved to see Gary looking so good. Alec would later tell me that he had been praying that cancer would not make Daddy look scary. God was extremely gracious in this regard, because even though he would endure horrible chemotherapy, Gary always looked pretty good, especially considering the circumstances. And this was not lost on Alec. He would thank God nightly for helping his daddy not look too sick.

We were gearing up for the pathology report, Gary was getting exercise, we were quoting Scripture, and anxiety was under control. Things were beginning to look up. Monday, April 11, Dr. Leach entered our room. He took a seat and then broke our hearts.

He said, "Gary, the report shows that the cancer is extremely aggressive. Though it wasn't in the lymph nodes in the front of your chest, all the lymph nodes in the left lung were saturated, as was the lymph node under your lung. Plus, you had positive margins for cancer at the site where your left lung was removed. Considering the aggressiveness of this cancer, it would be wishful thinking to hope that we caught it all or that it hasn't traveled all the way through your body. This type of cancer typically will attack a major organ next. It's extremely aggressive."

There was nothing but silence. I looked at Gary and his eyes were vacant. He looked away from me and started fixating on his IV.

"Gary?" I said, waiting for him to bring his eyes up to mine. "This news is really no different than the news we heard three weeks ago from Mark. Dr. Leach is a wonderful man and an amazing doctor, but he doesn't know that God won't heal you."

I continued, "Gary, a tsunami just hit Japan. It killed thousands of people, some of whom probably had cancer. They probably thought they were going to die of cancer but they went home by a giant tsunami wave instead. There could be someone reading our CaringBridge site right now who could go home before you. God is the author of our days, Gary, not cancer. Honey, listen to me. God told you to lean on me and walk in your healing. This was what He meant. We will fight the way God directs us. Do you understand?"

"But, Rosey, what does that mean?" he asked desperately.

"I don't know yet," I responded, "but we have to trust God. But Gary, I can't fight this battle for you. I can only walk alongside you. You have to walk with me in trust too."

Gary kept fixating on his IV. "Do you think the blood should be backing up like that?" he asked.

I was losing him. The mental game he had held onto so strongly was crumbling, he wasn't processing the information at all. It was the beginning of the most bizarre mental retreat I had ever seen. It was as if God put His two fingers right into Gary's ears, and from that moment on Gary would say, "They got all the cancer when they took out the lung, right?"

Dr. Leach stood up and came over to us. "Gary, you listen to Rosey now," he said. "Everything she said is correct. We are not done fighting. Rarely do we see someone in as good as shape as you. We will do everything in our power to help you get well and have victory."

Gary looked at Dr. Leach and then back at his IV. Dr.

Leach nodded at me and then left the room. I did not post the pathology report on CaringBridge—I needed time to process everything that was going on. Gary needed time too. Plus, my very bright engineer was beginning to "exit the building" mentally, and I was completely befuddled as to how I should support him.

At first I didn't know what to do but agree with him. I needed him to fight, so the last thing I wanted to do was remind him of his chances. I brought up the need to talk to a psychologist. Gary refused. I mean he absolutely *refused*. I needed the Lord like never before. "God, please direct our paths!"

Thankfully, God didn't make me wait long before He reminded me of something I had read years ago about not stripping people of their denial, hope, or faith because you never know how God is powering and protecting them. That was all it took. If Gary wasn't going to accept this diagnosis, then the heck if I would. I chose right then and there that I would follow his lead.

I told only a few select people about the actual diagnosis. If people would ask me what the pathology report said, my response was always, "Keep praying; we have a big fight on our hands." It sounds easy, doesn't it? Well, I can assure you, it wasn't. I know loved ones were frustrated with me, especially Gary's family. The only person I told in Gary's family was his older brother, Greg. I don't blame them for being frustrated with me either. I often prayed for forgiveness for not being completely forthright, but as long as Gary believed he was healed then I would protect his position.

Without God's strength, this is an impossible position to maintain. Satan attacked Gary and the boys with anxiety and fear. And he attacked me by trying to mentally destroy my resolve. The first of my many tests was twenty-four hours away, and it was a doozy. Gary continued to fixate on his IV and push his body physically.

STANDING IN TRUTH AND MOVING FORWARD

On the morning of the fourth day, Jody caught me in an upper walkway of the hospital lobby on my way up to see Gary. "Rosey, I just stopped by Gary's room. Can you sit with me a second?" she asked.

My whole body stiffened. "Sure," I said.

"Can you tell me what you heard Dr. Leach say?"

I wasn't going to play any games with her, so I was direct. "Jody, I know what he said and I know that Gary isn't processing the information. Is that what you want to talk to me about? Are you afraid we don't understand?"

"Well, yes," she said slightly taken back by my directness and, perhaps, by my slightly brittle tone. "It's very difficult news to receive," Jody said. "How are you doing?"

I tried desperately not to make eye contact with her. My mind was racing. How did I feel? Shouldn't I know? Should I be taking a personal inventory? I looked all around the busy hallway before I could bring my eyes to meet hers. "I don't even think I know how I'm doing right now," I finally responded. "My neighbor Mary gave me a card the night before the pathology report came back. She said that God prompted her to bring it over. The Scripture he gave her was

Psalm 112:7: 'He will have no fear of bad news; his heart is steadfast, trusting in the Lord.'"

Then I said, "When I read this verse I knew God was preparing us. Jody, we will not walk in fear—we *can't* walk in fear. We believe God wants to heal Gary. I know you must think this is crazy, but it is where we stand." I listened to myself say these words with conviction, but I knew in my spirit this was a tall order.

"Rosey, we see miracles every day," Jody said. "Sometimes it's a miracle of grace as we watch someone pass from this world to the next; sometimes it's a miracle of time when someone lives longer than expected. And sometimes it is a full healing. We work hard every day for the miracles we get to witness, and, yes, I believe God is at the center of each one." As she said this, her eyes were filled with compassion.

"Jody," I paused for a moment. "When the medical team reviewed the pathology report, what did Dr. Leach say was our time line?" (I was thinking, "Why, why, why had I asked that question?")

She took my hand. "A year from the diagnosis." We sat in silence for a minute as her words hung in the air. Jody continued, "You know, Rosey, over the years patients have taught us wonderful and honorable ways to help Gary walk through this part of his life journey. I have patients who have taken trips, had their family pictures taken, made memory quilts, videos—"

I took a deep breath and interrupted her. My mind was yelling no, but at the same time I was also listening to her. A family photo is a great idea before he gets too sick. I wonder if he would do a video for the boys? It was the beginning of my double-minded journey. My thoughts would often sound like this: "Yes! Praise God! He is healed, but if he isn't maybe I should get a friend started on a compilation of his favorite music."

"Jody, I truly thank you for walking through the process with us," I said, "but right now we just need to sit with this information for a while."

"I understand. When you are ready I have the name of a counselor for you and the boys, as well as for Gary. We will keep in touch." She gave me a hug and then got up to leave. She was so sweet and caring. Truly, if you had to have this type of conversation, you would want to have it with Jody. I felt so bad for hating her so much.

I walked downstairs to the lobby and began pacing back and forth. There were people having coffee in the lounge area, a new mom was holding her baby while waiting for her husband to pick her up, and then there was me pacing back and forth in the corner of the lobby in front of a huge window. The sounds of life around me were deafening. The belief of healing was being sucked right out of me. I fought back hard, I claimed Scripture, I claimed victory, yet Jody's, Mark's, and Dr. Leach's words kept ringing in my ears—"It might be nice to get a family picture done," "This is a very aggressive cancer," and "Get your affairs in order."

I was mentally breaking apart and my tears were uncontrollable. If I wasn't in the middle of a hospital lobby, I would have stomped my foot or thrown something. Mentally, I cried out, "Lord, help me. This battle is too much! Where is my help going to come from?"

God's response to this heartfelt cry? "Call Mary Lechtenberg." It came as clear as a bell.

I dialed Mary as fast as I could. Thankfully, she answered. Mary is a dear friend I had met years earlier when our boys were in kindergarten together at Bethany Academy. Mary and I are as opposite in personality types as two friends can be. She is reflective, quiet, peaceful, and disciplined—me, not so much. It was Mary who years ago opened up and encouraged my understanding of God's will to heal illness. Over the years I have been amazed by her wisdom, belief, and faith on the subject.

When she answered the phone, I blubbered about everything that had happened over the last forty-eight hours. "Mary, I'm not able to bear up under the attack. I know God's will is to heal Gary, but I can't keep all the medical results at bay. They said it's all over his body, it's not behaving like it should, and that we don't have long. Gary isn't mentally processing well, and today I can barely stand. How am I supposed to go into his room right now and be strong?"

"Oh, Rosey!" she said. "Oh my! Let me pray right now!"

I don't remember the whole prayer, just the first line: "God, wash over Rosey like a flowing river. Revive her spirit and…" As she prayed, I felt my strength fill. My tears dried up. I regained my composure. I felt my resolve return. The voices in my head were gone. Mary prayed life back into my very spirit. It was the first but it definitely wouldn't be the last time that I would need to lean on her faith to help me carry the weight of standing in healing.

Renewed, I went to Gary's room aware that I was an hour and a half later than he expected. Upon entering his room, I immediately noticed his deteriorating mental state. He was sullen, not really answering my questions. He just stared out the window. The hospital room felt dark and desperate. "Gary, I think we need to go home today instead of tomorrow," I said. Boy, did that bring him back into reality.

"What? Is that why you were so late, because you were getting things ready at home? Shouldn't we have discussed this? Where am I going to sleep?"

"No. And I don't know yet, but we need to get you out of here. Like now! Do you trust me?"

"Well, I guess I have to, but I think the hospital is the best place for me."

"That is precisely why we are leaving," I said. "What you need now is to get back to living."

"Let's see what Jody says. She was just here."

"I know, I ran into her in the hall. I think she will be OK with the decision. There is really no reason for you to stay here." God had restored me fully. It was time to fight His way, and suddenly I knew what my man needed. Within a few hours we were released and on our way out of the hospital. We were headed home, but we had one stop to make first.

The car ride was nothing short of horrible. Every bump and turn sent Gary reeling in pain. It felt like there were thousands of speed bumps in the parking garage alone. With him feeling every little movement of the car, it was inconceivable that I wasn't taking him straight home. Totally insensitive, right? If it sounds crazy reading it, then you can imagine the look on Gary's face when we drove past our exit.

"Rosey, why didn't you get off at our exit?" he asked. "Where are you going?"

"We are going on a little detour to the health food store," I said.

"Why are you taking me to the health food store? Rosey, are you trying to kill me? I just had my lung removed five days ago. I should still be in the hospital and you're taking me to the health food store?"

The written word can't possibly convey the emotion in his voice at that moment. Imagine booming, frantic, and slightly screechy, especially as he built up to his crescendo. You would never know he only had one lung.

"Yep, that is where I'm taking you," I said. "And you can do it. You were walking two miles a day in the hospital. Gary, remember I can't fight this battle for you. You are going to have to change your eating habits and I want you to see that you have options. We are going to take just one loop around the store," I said with more confidence than I felt. Internally, I was second-guessing myself too.

"Fine, but I am not pushing the cart or carrying out the groceries!" he said.

The health food store was just the boost we needed. We stopped and bought organic foods of all sorts. While we shopped, we discussed how to fight cancer from a diet perspective. True to my word, we left within thirty minutes, but that was all it took. I saw curiosity in my husband's eyes—and dare I say, hope? We were on our way back home in more ways than one.[3]

Being at home did wonders for his spirit, and that of our whole family. Yes, upon his arrival Angel, our dog, went crazy and the boys' excitement was at a fever pitch, but it did nothing but make him smile, proof that the love and joy of home are benefits that cannot be filled at the pharmacy window.

Gary's dad came for a visit the following day, and they walked half of a mile. This was in addition to the lunges and light dumbbell lifts he did. He also backed his pain meds down a bit. Though he was sore, he readily welcomed the company as people came over to say hi.

PERIOD TWO: THE FIGHT

It was time to prepare for period two: the fight. I had been in deep prayer about the next step of Gary's healing, and God had led me down a very specific path. Period two would be fought in the realm of the mind and the spirit. It began that day and it would last forever. This technically meant it would overlap with period three, which would involve dancing,

---

3   Note to all caregivers: it is important to know your patient. Gary is a competitor by nature, an athlete. Facing insurmountable challenges has always "jacked him up." He thrives on it. I pushed him because I know how Gary ticks. This is not a strategy I would suggest for everyone. In truth, many times my heart just wanted to hold and coddle him, but this was not about me. No, Gary needed a coach, not a nursemaid. Think Mickey from the *Rocky* movies, just with a better wardrobe and hopefully a little cuter. Can you hear the "Eye of the Tiger" playing in the background? Fortunately, this worked for me as well because there is a reason I didn't follow my sisters and mother into the field of nursing, because historically I'm not known for being the Florence Nightingale type.

hooting, hollering, and general celebration, because that would be when we received a diagnosis of "cured."

Period two opened with the philosophy of our whole family, and we hoped the whole team of those who were fighting along with us. The root of our philosophy can be found in Romans 8, where Paul writes, "For those who are according to the flesh set their minds on the things of the flesh, but those who are according to the Spirit, the things of the Spirit. For the mind set on the flesh is death, but the mind set on the Spirit is life and peace" (Romans 8:5–6).

We as a family had laid this cancer down at the foot of the cross. We knew that healing cancer was God's job, whether He chose to do that through a miracle or through medicine. Our job was to live in the present moment with our focus on Him. We knew that God was really good at what He does, and frankly who is going to mess with Him and win?

I also knew that Team Brausen was on board, but this very simple philosophy can be difficult to live out. It takes intentional effort; it takes capturing every thought and conforming it to the mind of Christ. For our family, it meant we kept our eyes fixed on God, not cancer. We came to the table with time in the Word, prayer, diet, exercise, and an attitude of gratitude. The rest is in God's court. And we can honestly tell you there is a certain peace that comes in complete surrender.

Chapter 6

No Time to Think, No Time to Pray

I am not sure I can accurately remember the month after Gary's surgery in great detail. What I do remember, however, is desperately trying to keep life normal for the boys, and, in hindsight, for Gary and myself as well. Science fair projects were due, piano recitals were coming up, spring choir and band concerts were on the horizon, and mix in there my job, doctor appointments, and processing our new life—days were a complete blur during this time.

There are two things I do distinctly remember from this time: Gary and I made a conscious and united choice not to let cancer be an excuse for missing life—not for us, and not for Bennett or Alec either. During this period of time we often fought the temptation to use the "cancer card," especially when it came to the boys' pending science fair projects. It would be so much easier to just say we couldn't get to projects because of, you know, cancer.

As we were quickly finding out, life can be difficult and people always have two choices before them: they can either fight or flee. We wanted the boys to see staying in the fight is hard but better in the long run. Did we make life more difficult for ourselves? Probably so. Do we regret it? Not at all. Would we respond the same way again? I don't think so, since it was all kind of silly and dramatic, but it did help us keep the boys' minds distracted.

For his part, Gary worked diligently on body restoration. He weaned off pain medication weeks earlier than expected. He also made sure to stay in the Word of God. To keep anxiety at bay, he claimed victory moment by moment. For the boys, homework was completed (with more than a wee bit of grace from their teachers on late assignments), sporting practices were made, we talked about our feelings often, and we tried to be honest with each other, even though we weren't always successful.

Gary's older brother, Greg, came for a visit and helped Gary prepare his mental game. It was so nice to have Greg around—he was a comrade in arms and noticed Gary's emotional state immediately. Greg's daily text messages, along with my sister Donna and brother-in-law Kemper, and my sister-in-law Pam, and our friend Bill Zimmer, would become Gary's lifeline. They all became Gary's personal sounding boards, cheerleaders, and support system. Their daily or weekly communication brought him so much joy. They truly sustained him and kept him in the land of the living. There are no words for the amount of gratitude I have in my heart for each and every one of them.

During these first days, I will always be thankful for the gift of laughter, for our house was blessed with it abundantly. Later, as chemo raged through Gary's body, it would be harder and harder to laugh. We learned that Gary would begin chemotherapy on May 9 and it would end on July 11. There would be a total of four sessions. His reaction to the chemo was yet to be learned, but typically patients experienced nausea and fatigue, but no hair loss. This was a great relief to Bennett and Alec.

Bennett said it best: "Mom, seriously, the three of us have enormous heads. You don't understand because you have a pinhead. For Dad, Alec, and me, being bald would not be pretty!" (You have to imagine the hand gestures, head nodding for emphasis, and the I'm-not-kidding facial expression to really capture the seriousness of this topic to Bennett.)

Gary and Alec were right there with him, trying to get me to understand. Actually, my greatest laugh was when I suggested on the off chance that Gary would lose his hair, they could both shave their heads in support. Their horror makes me laugh out loud even to this day.

The second and more important conscious choice we made was following a prompt by the Lord—repentance. As Gary was feeling better and regaining his strength, the Lord kept prompting me about the importance of repentance and its role in healing. I remembered Scriptures such as:

> Therefore, confess your sins to one another, and pray for one another so that you may be healed. The effective prayer of a righteous man can accomplish much (James 5:16).

And,

> Bless the LORD, O my soul and forget none of His benefits; who pardons all your iniquities, who heals all your

diseases; who redeems your life from the pit... (Psalm 103:2–4).

I am not a theologian or a pastor, but my very simple childlike understanding of why repentance is important boils down to this: First, I know God to be all holy; otherwise, how else could He be God? He simply can't be in the presence of sin. Something has to cover the sin in our lives in order for us to be in His presence.

Second, God is a relational God. He sent His Son to die on the cross as the ultimate sacrifice for our sins. When Jesus died on the cross and shed His physical blood for us, He became our mercy seat. Therefore, we no longer need blood sacrifices or priests to be our intercessors in order to connect us with God. Upon His death, resurrection, and victory over Satan, Jesus sent us the Holy Spirit through whom God now has a personal relationship with us directly.

Third, any type of sin sits in a space between God and us. Sin simply can't be in the presence of pure holiness. If this is confusing, think opposing polar forces like the positive and negative properties of a magnet. Therefore, when we have sin in our lives, we actually build a wall between God and us. This happens not because He doesn't love us in our sin but because our sins can't coexist in the same space with Him. If we want to get as close to God as possible, then we need to pay more attention to repentance. Unfortunately, the truth is that we sin a lot, either consciously or unconsciously, so there can be layer upon layer of sin between God and us.

This all seems easy enough, but God was going to teach

Gary and me how to confess in a whole new way. Here is how we started. We sat down on the couch together with a notebook and a pen one evening. I started with a random typical sin that I thought might be safe. "Gary, have you ever been critical of anyone?" I asked.

"I don't think so—at least, I know I don't make a habit of it."

"Yeah, me neither," I said. "It's not usually my thing. Let's just pray and see if God brings anything to mind." (Are you laughing at our lack of self-awareness yet?)

Well, it didn't take long for God to give us our first example. Gently, I heard in my spirit, "Have you ever judged someone else's work performance? How about parenting style or financial responsibility?" In short order, God brought to my memory several examples. ("OK. I get it, Lord. We can take it from here.") Gary and I spent an hour on this one sin alone. We confessed, we struggled, we asked for forgiveness, and we gave forgiveness. And when we were done, I burned our notes.

We did this for several nights in a row. Jealousy, envy, unforgiveness, bitterness, selfishness, lust—you name it, we tried to cover it. I learned a lot about my husband in those nights. He was so transparent, so real. He didn't hide from his ugliness; rather, he confronted it. By his example of transparency I grew in trust and was able to be more transparent as well. He was seriously in danger of making me love him even more.

Our feelings for each other were the exact opposite response you would expect from such an exercise. When you think of telling someone your ugly stuff, do you think it is going to make you more endearing? Of course not. Typically, we are afraid it will repel others. If they knew the real truth about us, we would be rejected and shunned—definitely not forgiven. As humans we tend to be more prone to conditional love standards, which is one of the reasons we have difficulty believing and trusting the unconditional love of God. It's a very foreign concept to us.

I imagine this is why God wants us to confess our sins to Him. The more we trust Him with our icky stuff, the closer He draws to us and the more complete and intimate our relationship with Him becomes. It is an honor to be allowed into someone's dark places, a very sacred privilege indeed.

What God also put on our hearts during this time was the importance of needing to forgive and forget what we each heard about the other person. Luckily for me, this was easy for Gary because he barely remembers those nights at all, let alone our times of confession. For me it was equally easy because I don't like to entertain icky stuff—mine or anyone else's. I can't get rid of that junk fast enough.

A SECOND OPINION

As Gary healed from surgery, we were given the opportunity to go for a second opinion at Dana-Farber Cancer Institute in Boston. The cancer was acting very oddly, and our medical team thought in our case Dana-Farber would be the best place to go. If there was something new out there, some new type of cancer treatment, then Dana-Farber would know about it. We were so thankful for the opportunity, yet, at the same time, nobody wants to be battling a cancer that Dana-Farber is interested in either.

It took a herculean effort to make this appointment happen. There was just a short window of time between the time Gary was well enough to fly and the beginning of chemotherapy. The mighty Team Brausen prayer machine got on their knees and doors began to open. Our medical team was able to make an appointment, my sister Kathy and her husband, Kemper, bought us airline tickets, and my sister Terri stayed with the boys. Greg's in-laws put us up in Boston, and within seven days of initial discussion we found ourselves in the lobby of Dana-Farber.

It had been a whirlwind week. We were blessed with a visit from Gary's older brother, Greg, from California, a chemo "test drive" meeting, Mother's Day, science fair projects, and ultimately a trip to Boston. Needless to say, we arrived in Boston a little wilted. From the moment we stepped into Greg's in-laws' home, their wonderful and generous hospitality began to revive us immediately. They were the most gracious and giving hosts. Ellen was a cancer survivor and mentored Gary through the whole visit.

We had our meeting at Dana-Farber, and from the moment we entered that facility we were humbled with our own insignificance. The place was beyond words. We had never seen so much hope and fight simultaneously existing together in such close proximity. One might think they were the same thing, and perhaps they are.

As we entered the registration room, we were greeted by the music of a gentleman playing the piano in the lobby. We sat and gathered our emotions for a moment, just listening to his soothing music. We approached him to thank him for making a very difficult entry so much easier. He stopped for a minute and said, "That is why I come and play. My real job is a few floors up. I don't write this music down, it just comes out of my heart." He was all of twenty-eight years old.

In the lobby we witnessed the effects of cancer on humanity. It has no mercy, no preference. It infiltrates every culture, every age, and all economies; it does not discriminate. Yet, from where we sat in the lobby, it was equally evident that cancer wasn't winning—it was just trying very hard. Gary and I will never look at another individual again without wondering what burden they may be carrying.

We met with our Dana-Farber team, who could not have been more professional and compassionate. They were also highly complementary of our Minnesota team. They confirmed that we were on the right path, and they said they would be responding exactly the same way. They also confirmed that the cancer that was found in Gary's left lung was acting oddly.

Honestly, we were hoping that Dana-Farber would offer a simpler plan for the second phase of our journey. They didn't, but they did confirm what we already knew—our team in Minnesota was excellent. They have no idea how right they were. I wanted to explain the depth of Team Brausen to them, and I don't just mean the medical team. But tears were welling and I was without words.

All of our time there was extremely satisfying—not just comforting but actually satisfying. We had confirmation of our gut intuition about our team at Abbott. God had truly been walking with us all along, taking care of every detail before we even understood what we needed. I wanted to shout out, "See, that's how our God works!" to anybody who would listen, but He does not need our trumpeting. He just loves that we know and trust Him.

While at Dana-Farber, I was touched by a quote I had read from Sidney Farber: "The purpose of life is to spend it on something that outlives you; no man finds his ultimate end in himself, but does so by sharing with others."[4] Team Brausen had shared their time, the prayers, their food, their treasures, their heart, and, most importantly, their faith with us throughout this journey. They had impacted our family in such a profound way that it had changed our trajectory.

The Dana-Farber medical team was extremely kind. They encouraged Gary to keep fighting. They filled him with hope. Yes, if the cancer came back there were things they could try. But the emphasis was on the *if*. Even though I was very satisfied with our visit, I was also slightly frustrated with our situation. Because of Gary's mental state, I did not ask them the questions I would have typically asked. My guardian angels must have been exhausted after that visit because everything in my body was screaming for more information, yet I didn't press them at all. They must have used heaven's armies to help me hold my tongue.

When we returned home, without Gary's knowledge I asked for a copy of the Dana-Farber report. They concurred with Dr. Leach's conclusion. In their opinion, the cancer

4   Miller, D. R. (2006), A tribute to Sidney Farber – the father of modern chemotherapy. British Journal of Haematology, 134: 20–26. doi: 10.1111/j.1365-2141.2006.06119.x.

would most likely return and, when it did, they had a few alternative types of chemo to try to extend life. Reading this broke my heart. I gave the original pathology report and the Dana-Farber report to yet a third oncologist my sister Donna knew. He didn't pull any punches either. In his opinion, Gary didn't have a chance.

I was crushed with all of this new information. Why hadn't I followed Gary's lead early on when he decided not to seek information out about the cancer? He stopped going to the Internet looking for more and more answers. Instead, he took a single-minded position: he would beat this thing—the odds didn't matter. His case would be different. ("Why, oh why, Lord, do I keep taking my eyes off You?")

It was going to be harder for me to stand in healing, because now I was going to have to stare down three medical opinions plus what our neighbor had witnessed under the microscope. I envied Gary's position. There was no place for me to hide except in the shadow of the wings of God (Psalm 91:1).

A few days after we returned home from Boston, God woke me up in the middle of the night. "Rosey," He said. I was groggy, but it didn't take me long to figure out who was talking to me. Silent tears ran down my cheeks immediately.

"Oh, Lord, I'm so sorry," I prayed. "I am having trouble standing in belief. All the doctors are saying the news isn't good." (Isn't it funny that I felt the need to bring God up to date?)

The Holy Spirit brought to my memory the story of Daniel's three friends—Shadrach, Meshach, and Abednego. He reminded me of how they not only needed to climb the staircase but they needed to go into the fire. Then I heard, "And you will not smell of smoke."

"Lord, does this mean Gary will live?" I implored.

"Just remember not everyone is able to climb the staircase," He continued. "Some of the guards died mounting the stairs because the heat was so intense. I am with you all through the journey and you will not smell of smoke."

"But, Lord, what does 'not smelling of smoke' mean? Does Gary live?" There was no response—just silence. I sat in the warmth of His presence for a little longer as He tended to my spirit, then I retreated back into sleep.

The next morning I bolted out of bed and ran for my Bible. Sure enough, reading through Daniel 3, I saw that verse 27 says, "And there was no smell of fire on them." That small charred piece of paper given to Gary from Fred months earlier had new significance to Gary and me after that night. We put it in a frame. It was our symbol of hope from the Lord. Gary would walk through this fire and not smell of smoke.

BEING DOUBLE MINDED IS DISASTROUS

The Lord's kindness to me that night was what I used to fight my own mental battle. For the next four months to Gary, Bennett, Alec, and most of Team Brausen, I was unfaltering in my belief in Gary's healing, but the audience I gave Satan in my private thoughts depleted my much-needed strength.

Every morning before my feet hit the floor, I put on my biblical armor, I quoted Scripture over myself, and I reminded myself of the signs that God had showed me, yet I yielded to doubt and what-if scenarios again and again. I entertained thoughts of what it would be like to be a widow—so I repented. I imagined Gary's funeral—and then I repented. I wondered how I would support the boys by myself—and then I repented again. I fell again and again, and I repented over and over. My repentance was typically pretty simple: "Lord, forgive me for taking my eyes off You and entertaining the alternative." God's grace was sufficient.

You might be thinking it would be impossible not to entertain such thoughts during a time like this. I would agree. What God spoke into my heart and gently convicted me of was that my mental wonderings lacked purpose and they lacked Him. They weren't life-giving thoughts; they didn't change the circumstances of the day. They were thoughts of a possible future, but they lacked God.

Entertaining such scenarios began to splinter my mental wholeness. The more I allowed my mind to wander into tomorrow, the more difficult it was to live and pray in belief for today. You simply can't pray for healing while you are planning a funeral. I now have new understanding of the importance and discipline of adhering to this Scripture: "Therefore do not *worry about tomorrow*, for tomorrow will worry about itself. Each day has *enough trouble of its own*" (Matthew 6:34 NIV).

God answered my humanness in His pure God style. He spread His glory and kindness all over my family and me. He showered us with prayers from Team Brausen. Pam Nickman sent six different prayers when she felt God touch her heart to pray for our family.

I vividly remember this one because it came the morning after a particularly difficult night, when I was feeling exhaustion in every part of my body. God had brought me to her mind this particular day, so she penned this prayer and sent it to me.

Dear heavenly Father, I ask for You to quiet Rosey's heart. Give her peace to bask in the wonderful weather we are having and the slower pace of summer. May there be many moments when she can sit at Your feet and soak in all You want to tell her in this day. I ask for many moments of fun and closeness for their family this summer. I ask for Gary to have energy to accomplish those things You have planned for him. Also, please continue to grow Gary in Your Word and give him insight into Your ways for the journey he has ahead. Please, Lord, continue to heal Gary's body and keep the cancer at bay. Please give wisdom to the doctors, nurses, and any caregivers that Gary and Rosey come into contact with.

Also, may all these caregivers see the strong faith they have in You, and may You open up many doors for them to share about their faith during this journey. Also, Lord, I ask You to keep this family close to You. Where Satan tries to feed lies or instill fear, I ask You to help this family claim Your Word and keep strong. Bless Rosey with rest, peace, and joy during the days ahead. Keep them focused always on You and help them to rest always in Your peace, perfection, and plan for the days ahead. Please help them to know You are walking before them each step of the way.

In Your name I pray. Amen.

God knew I needed a pick-me-up, so He sent Pam's prayer. When I was the most disappointed in myself for not bearing up well and entertaining doubtful thoughts, God grew my faith and confidence when He brought this Scripture to mind: "But the Helper, the Holy Spirit, whom the Father will send in My name, He will teach you all things, and bring to your remembrance all that I said to you" (John 14:26).

Then the Holy Spirit reminded me of Jesus carrying His cross and falling three times along the way. He also reminded me that He called Simon out of the crowd to help Jesus. Jesus fell only three times; I probably fell about three thousand times. But it was clear God was present in my battle, and whether I fell three thousand or three million times, He was right there picking me back up through many different ways, but mostly through the prayers and kindness of Team Brausen.

As time went on, God shored up my weaknesses, my heart and mind became more united in the belief of Gary's healing, and I began to fall less and less. This must have really ticked Satan off because he was going to war even harder for my mind. Thankfully, I didn't know this yet. Ignorance can truly be bliss at times.

Gary had entered a fairly good mental place, all things notwithstanding. He was in control of the anxiety. The denial of the severity of this cancer was deep, which gave him a measure of peace. He even told me he didn't think we needed Team Brausen to be praying anymore. "Ahh…yes, we do," was my response.

Chapter 7

Chemo and Miracles

You cannot estimate prayer power. Prayer is as vast as
God because He is behind it. Prayer is as mighty as God
because He has committed Himself to answer it.
—Leonard Ravenhill[5]

Being prayed for is an essential part of any healing, whether
it is emotional, spiritual, or physical. There are of course
thousands of ways to pray, but the times that brought
Gary and me the most peace were the gatherings when friends
would lay hands on Gary. Gary received prayer in this fashion
on three different occasions: twice early on in our journey,
and the third time came after radiation. Each time God met
him in a different way, but His timing was always perfect.

The first time Gary was prayed for was right after he was
diagnosed with cancer. The Allisons and Russells are coworkers of mine at Bethany Academy. Over the years they have been
hugely instrumental in teaching me about the importance of
worship as an amplifier of faith. They are spiritual warriors of
the highest level, so when they invited us to a worship night at
their church's youth group, we immediately said yes.

---

5   Leonard Ravenhill, *Why Revival Tarries* (Bloomington, MN: Bethany House
    Publishers, 1959, 1987), 151.

At the end of worship, all of the teens gathered around Gary and lifted him up to the Lord in prayer and song for over an hour. My sweet husband just wept and wept. God met him in his spirit and comforted and prepared him for the journey that was ahead. This was a beautiful and life-giving time for both of us. We had never met any of these kids before, yet they prayed over Gary like he was their dearest friend.

The second time Gary was prayed for was right before chemotherapy began. Mary and her husband, Scott, hosted a prayer gathering of a few friends from Bethany Academy. It was such a sweet and tender time. I don't think anyone is truly ready for chemotherapy and all of its unknowns, but the prayer time with our friends reminded us that we were walking into this season covered in the prayers of the faithful.

During this season was the first time God brought to mind a Scripture found in Luke 10:19: "Behold, I have given you authority to tread on serpents and scorpions, and over all the power of the enemy, and nothing will injure you." This Scripture helped Gary and me stand when he was battling the effects of chemotherapy. Throughout the whole process, Gary's blood work stayed within the normal ranges, which was a miracle in and of itself.

Our medical team was amazing in how they prepared us for chemo. We watched a video, toured the infusion room, and learned that not everyone receives the same amount or type of chemo, and that chemo actually responds differently in each person. They went to great strides to take the "fear" out of chemo, although it was an impossible task.

Gary was scheduled for four treatments of the cisplatin and

alimta cocktail, one treatment every three weeks. That doesn't sound like much, but four treatments are about all the body can take. Gary would later say it was like getting within inches of death and then being brought back to life four times over.

Our first appointment was scheduled for Monday, May 17, at 9:00 a.m. That morning the Brausen house was in full swing. The boys were getting ready for school and Gary was making himself very, very busy. He did the dishes, swept the floors, cleaned the counters, looked through the paper, and folded the laundry. He wouldn't look at me at all that morning. I waited and watched the clock, pretty confident we were not the only patients to run late for their first chemo appointment. There would be forgiveness.

We were scheduled to leave our home at 8:15 a.m., but at 8:50 a.m. I picked up the keys and walked to the door in silence. Gary simply followed. On the drive we listened to music and held hands, but we didn't say a word.

When we finally arrived and went to the oncology floor, Gary couldn't bring himself to sit in the chair and get started. It was the element of the unknown that stopped him in his tracks. He didn't know how his body was going to respond, and neither did anyone else. In hindsight he thinks he handled this poorly, even though I tell him he handled it with courage and transparency. Who knows how anyone is going to handle sitting in a chemo chair for eight hours straight until they actually do it. For me, they would probably need restraints.

Eight hours later we were leaving the oncology floor and on our way to Alec's first baseball game of the season. Gary didn't feel any different; it would be another forty-eight hours before he felt the effects of the first round of chemo. Though it was hard, we weren't surprised when it hit—we were well prepared.

GARY DRAWS CLOSER TO THE LORD

What cancer, chemo, and radiation couldn't take away was Gary's desire to lean into God during this time. God uses absolutely everything to bring us closer to Him, and He used this time of vulnerability in Gary to radically draw him into relationship with Himself. Gary explains it best himself in these two back-to-back CaringBridge entries. Here are his thoughts:

June 1, 2011

If I am not wrong, the definition of a blog is an entity that you update every day. Between the difficult content of this second post, my underestimation of the side effects of the treatment, and the huge physical and emotional swings, I have not been able to update this site as frequently as I would like. My apologies for the delay in this second post and leaving you all hanging so long. Well, here goes number two.

In my first post last week, I attempted to say thank you for how I have been so blessed over the past three months. One group of folks I forgot to mention were the folks who have accompanied me on my many walks. These walks have provided not only a physical fitness outlet for me, which is much needed as I heal and recover, but also an emotional outlet as well. My sincerest thanks to these folks for their time and their engaging conversation.

Also in my first post, I mentioned that what has occurred over the past three months somehow was the best thing that has ever happened to me. Some skeptics might think that it is because it has provided an excuse for me to take some time off of work. I am here to say that nothing could be further from the truth, and I trust that my colleagues at Seagate will back me up on this, for I greatly miss working and cannot wait to return.

This next concept was at first very hard to understand for me and will be equally challenging for me to convey. It is certainly not a new concept or something I invented, as famous people have uttered similar things in the past. One instance that comes to mind occurred on July 4, 1939, and no, I was not alive to hear it myself. This is when Lou Gehrig told a full house at Yankee Stadium during his famous farewell speech that he considered himself "the luckiest man on the face of this earth." Today I understand his sentiments perfectly.

To best explain all of this, I am going to start with where I was before all of this came down in March of 2011. For just over fifty years, I always considered myself a "good person," which to me meant that I was a good dad, a good husband, a good family member, a good friend, and a good employee. I went to church on Sundays and said my prayers on most nights. I rarely swore with the exception of when I was golfing, tried to keep my word when I committed to something, and did my best not to hold grudges against family and/or friends. I did place value in some material possessions, such as cars, clothing, and watches, and was guilty of an extreme obsession with the game of hockey. With the exception of the material idolization, sounds like the ingredients of a decent person, right?

Not really, based on what I know now. What has changed for me is a spiritual awakening like I have never experienced before. I thought that I had similar experiences before, but I was wrong, as this is the real deal. What God showed me in the early part of last week was how my life was very self-involved.

I was present in my friendships, marriage, and as a father, but not engaged. Basically, I was there in body but not spirit. Facing myself full-on—the good, the bad, and the ugly—left me with a pure love of God deep in my spirit and the removal of fear of death, which I think I must have been afraid of for most of my life. After this awakening, many things have changed with me. To say that these changes are in place 24/7 would not be true as I am still a human and continue to sin even through this experience. What has changed for me is a much tighter connection with God than I ever had before.

I have learned that in order to hear or see Him, I must pay attention. As my awareness of Him is awakening, so is my amazement of His faithfulness; when God is trying to teach me something, He orchestrates situations that are tailor-made for what I have needed to learn. Many of you through your words and prayers have been His human teachers.

With this tighter relationship comes a true

appreciation of each and every moment, conversation, encounter, and experience. Hugs feel better, everything smells better (especially lilacs), and you truly begin to appreciate the smaller things in life, such as awesome cloud formations after storms, birds building nests, and many things I took for granted before.

Such a change does not go unnoticed, however, especially at home. For quite a few years, Rosey and I have maintained a very loving marriage but we had settled into a routine of polite agreement on many fronts and little confrontation; the results being few disagreements but also a harmony that lacked depth, which we all know is not good. Since this illness hit our home, the dynamics of our marriage needed to adjust very quickly. Now we take more time to go deeper, to fight a little (she can be feisty), and to work harder at honest compromise. As a father, I am more engaged than ever before in the day-to-day parenting of Ben and Alec, whom I cherish more than anything; already the rewards of being an engaged husband and father are better than I had imagined.

Hopefully I have adequately and transparently shared my experience.

I want to go through this process as open and honest as possible. A polished, perfect life holds such little value for me anymore. This illness has afforded me the time to adjust my priorities and focus on what is truly important. I finally realized I was casual in many important things and passionate about things that truly do not matter in the long run. I am very thankful for this teaching, as it has improved my life immeasurably, and for my God who waited so patiently for me to learn them.

And then again on June 7, 2011, Gary wrote:

Dear Team Brausen,

For many years, Rosey has heard God talking to her. Before my spiritual journey began in earnest, I was skeptical. I mean, I am an engineer and I deal mostly in the tangible.

This was quite a leap for me; listening for something that you cannot see, touch, or feel. Are you kidding me? As I progressed in my relationship with God, I got more and more intrigued with this notion to the point of wanting to hear Him myself. So I began asking questions of Rosey, as well as Bennett and Alec because they are quite gifted in this regard as well.

They would tell me and I would try it out. It seemed that the harder I tried the quieter it became. I was frustrated and an element of skepticism remained. Then, during this journey, everything changed. Over the past week, there have been two instances (one at home and one at Caribou) where information came pouring out of my head at such a rate that I could not even remember half of what was being said. What was being told to me was some of the coolest stuff I have ever had in my head, but the problem was that I wanted to remember it later but could not as there was just so much of it. I first thought that I was really coming up with some good stuff myself but then realized there was no possible way I could think of so much good stuff, so fast.

I finally realized who was doing the talking, and it was not me. I think that God is making up for many years of me not listening. Last night it started happening again, and I decided to try something a little different. As I lay in bed, the information came pouring out in huge quantities again, so I grabbed an envelope from one of the many cards I have received (yes, I have read and kept them all) and started scribbling the ideas I heard onto it. I did not care about penmanship, as I might have in the past, and just concentrated on capturing the content because this was the most important thing. As I wrote, I noticed that the ideas stopped flowing, suggesting that if your brain is doing anything else, you cannot hear what He is saying.

I walked back into the bedroom, placed the half-scribbled envelope on the nightstand, and turned off the light. After turning off the light and settling my brain again, the ideas began flowing again like a gusher. So I turned the light back on, wrote the ideas down, and turned out the light again. This process of hearing, flicking on the light, writing, and turning the light off occurred a dozen times that evening. I have never experienced anything like this before. Needless to say, I did not sleep well but it did not matter as this was another truly life-changing event.

After last night, I played back some other instances

in my past where life-changing ideas all of a sudden popped in my head. There was a situation a few years ago when my car caught fire after driving for a while, and not believing that my beloved Altima was on fire, I finally heard in my head, "Pull over into the Bloomington Post Office parking lot and check this out." At the time, I thought, "Wow, what a great idea I just had." I now know the true source of this brilliant idea.

So, does it take a life-altering event to begin hearing God speak to you? I do not think so. If not, then what does it take? Here is what I have learned after my personal experiences and after talking to each member of my immediate family:

1. He decides when to speak. So far for me, the information has come unsolicited. The harder I worked to listen, the less I heard.
2. He will speak at anytime, anyplace. Bennett says he hears God in his room all of the time. He gives him Scripture verses to look up, and, sure enough, many of his thoughts and questions are answered within the Scripture verses he hears. So He also may speak to you in the same location or through Scripture.
3. Having a close relationship with Him improves your ability to recognize His voice, because He has been talking to you your whole life.
4. For me, He is louder when my mind is uncluttered and quiet. This is really difficult in this hectic world of ours, and it is probably why kids are so

much better at it. Who besides me has their best ideas in the shower, in a bathroom stall, on a beach, or in a secluded spot up north?

5. All my good ideas and information have been undoubtedly His. I spent a lot of time taking credit for them myself. If you can learn anything from my experience at all, when you have a good idea don't waste time being too full of yourself.

6. If my case is at all typical, and you have not heard from Him in a while, keep pen and paper close by because it may be a gusher when He speaks. To be ready, keep a notebook on your nightstand just in case.

7. What has been equally difficult to understand for me is that we can also hear the other guy. The voice sounds the same but the message is full of despair, ugliness, and fear. During my worst days my head was full of fearful, self-loathing thoughts. As I understand this process, I am realizing that I don't have to listen to these thoughts. They are not of God. They do not come from me.

Rosey has been using the word "discernment" for a long time. I am beginning to discern the content of what I hear against what I know of the character of God. If it is life giving and beneficial then it's from God; if not, I ignore it. Funny thing since my epiphany, I have heard much less of the negative junk. It is truly freeing. Rosey and Bennett also say that you can judge the content of your message against what the Bible says…it's all in there. I must admit I am only beginning to crack open the "big book." I am sure I will understand this step as I read the book more.

My hope is that my experiences and what I have learned can help you all in some way.

GOD FAITHFULLY SUSTAINS US WITH ACTS OF KINDNESS AND A LITTLE REPRIMAND

Gary's increasing relationship would prove important as we went deeper into the chemo treatments. Chemo robbed Gary of his body and his ability to mentally process. The previous entries took us days to write, and they were at the beginning of his journey. By the last chemo treatment, his thoughts were often garbled and out of order. In the cancer world they call this chemo-brain.

For the kids and me it was the most difficult thing we had to watch him suffer through. By the end of his last chemo treatment, Gary went from benching a hundred and eighty-five pounds to hardly being able to lift five-pound dumbbells, from completing a duathlon to taking an hour to walk around the block. He had lost a total of twenty-five pounds, which I kindly keep for him around my middle.

His bipolar outbursts were the worst to handle. God was faithful to even use his erratic emotional state to stretch Gary and, dare I say, myself, but in a completely different manner.

One day Gary and I went out for a walk around the block, which is exactly one mile long. We had been walking for almost an hour, so you can get a good idea of the pace we were going. You can also probably get a picture of my husband's drive.

As we rounded the corner toward our home, we passed the house of our dear friends Linda and Larry. Over the previous year, our families had a series of miscommunications. Both our families were struggling in our own respective ways, and we had allowed little misunderstandings to build up over time. As we passed by their house, Gary said spitefully, "Look, I bet Linda is looking out her window happy that I am suffering and sick."

I was shocked at what came out of his mouth. My reply was firm and swift, "Gary Brausen, I don't care if you have cancer or not. You are never allowed to entertain such thoughts or utter them about anyone. That is simply the meanest thing you could say about anybody, and especially Linda! She would never think nor say something so mean spirited. This is just not you, and in the name of Jesus Christ this grudging spirit can just get behind you!"

Gary was silent for a few more steps, but I could tell by how he held his head he was still holding onto past hurts and they were festering. When we got home, Gary sat down exhausted by our walk and his emotional outburst. He was struggling in so many ways. My heart was breaking for him. And yet I was also a little ticked off at what he had said.

He was so weak and out of sorts. I started mentally tallying what he had eaten up to that point and it wasn't a lot, "Gary what are you hungry for? You need to eat something." His only reply was that all of the sudden he had an intense craving for fresh-cut, cold watermelon.

This was a new craving and, unfortunately, I was already

running late to pick up the kids, so there was no way I could go to the store and get him some. I would be home within the hour, however, and then I could get it for him.

Waiting on top of everything else seemed like an impossibility for Gary, and he let me know the level of his disappointment, but he was too weak to drive himself. There were no other options.

As we were bantering back and forth, the doorbell rang. When I opened the door, I started to giggle. There was Linda with a bowl of fresh-cut, cold watermelon. After I thanked her, I gave the bowl to Gary and told him it was from Linda. He was speechless. I said, "Gary, God just gave you a little spanking—God style. I wouldn't press Him again if I were you. Let go of the hurt, anger, and lies, and stop listening to the voice of resentment. It will eat you alive."

Then I continued, "As much as the Lord is grace filled, you need to understand what it means to fear Him as well. He won't stand for you to be mean-spirited toward anybody. It's not His nature and we are supposed to be conforming ourselves to Him."

One of the many beautiful attributes of Gary is his teachable spirit and transparency. You would think that he would be embarrassed to have this story included in this book, but it is the story he shares most often and he insisted it be represented.

Only a God-designed lesson can pack that kind of punch. Gary continued to have many bipolar responses as he traveled through treatment, but each time he was quick to make an apology. When he asked forgiveness, it was easier on all of us to help him carry this burden. Easier, yes, but I did go to extreme efforts to keep the kids out of the house or busy doing projects.

I needn't have worried about the boys as much as I did—their hearts were set on God, and the love they have for their daddy was it's own type of shield. In fact, Alec at one point wanted me to share with Team Brausen what he had been doing to help his dad fight cancer.

He said, "Mom, when I pray for Dad, I think of the Pac-Man game. I imagine all the cancer cells we can't even see running around, going crazy, thinking they are invisible. Then I give my Pac-Man guy night vision goggles so he can see them uncloaked. Once the cancer cells know they have been discovered, they start running in fear—but it doesn't matter because my Pac-Man is really hungry and faster than them.

"When Dad is feeling sick, I know it's because the Pac-Man guy is sick to his stomach from eating so many cells. I know I am right because when we were at Fleet Farm (one of his favorite stores) I saw a Pac-Man fireworks set…and that was God telling me I was on the right track because He knows how much I love fireworks and He knew I would see that set and put it all together."

Then he said, "Plus, Mom, each time Dad has chemo, I think God is just letting out more Pac-Man guys. Cancer doesn't have a chance in this game. Can we go back and get that fireworks set? I think that would help Dad too."

The next morning after I posted this story on our Caring-Bridge site, our neighbor Pat had the Pac-Man fireworks set on our doorstep. We still have the spent Pac-Man firework proudly displayed on our shelf to this day.

MORE CHEMO TREATMENTS

Typically, the week after a chemo treatment was the worst, and for Gary how he responded to the chemo aftermath was different each time. Each treatment brought its own type of hell. There were never two alike. However, except for the second treatment, he would drastically turn a corner and start to climb out of the hole he had entered around day seven. Because of the effects of the second chemo treatment, we almost didn't make chemo treatment number three or four. Here are four consecutive CaringBridge entries that put words to Gary's nightmare.

Entry 1: June 21, 2011

Hi Team Brausen,

Team, your captain has taken a pretty good-sized hit with this last treatment session. He was given an antibiotic for his four-alarm cold, which relieved some of the symptoms, but the cold is still very present and active. The cold led into a series of styes on his left eye that have clustered together, causing him intense pain and eye puffiness, and even though the fatigue brought on by treatment is lifting, he still can't sleep due to the coughing. All in all, this has left him more than a little discouraged and so tired of the whole process. Our next treatment is Monday and he is questioning very strongly whether or not he will participate. Our oncologist will help him make that call on Monday.

Do I need to even say we need your prayers? Well, we do. Please also pray for protection for Ben and Al, as watching their dad suffer has been very difficult this past week. Yet, over the last four months I have been so thankful that both the boys have been gifted with a quick wit and easy laughter that helps them stay resilient.

Most things don't translate well in print, but I think you can capture this little pearl.

Upon hearing Gary link several choice words together during a particularly low point, Alec raised his eyebrows, pursed his lips, tilted his head, and said, "Well, we know that the treatment hasn't affected Dad's intellect. He still has very good sentence structure, even using those words…most people just use *those* types of words one at a time."

Entry 2: June 26, 2011

Dearest Team Brausen,

When I said, "My foot is slipping," your love, O LORD, supported me! When anxiety was great within me, your consolation brought joy to my soul! (Psalm 94:18–19 NIV).

What a difference a day can make. I say a day because from the evening of my last post Gary finally slept through the night and he has continued to do so even as I write this post. His eye began healing that very night, and with the sleep came a return of Gary. I actually wept when I received his text Thursday night while I was at Bennett's game. He told me that he visited with a few friends who had stopped by, placed the garbage out at the curb, and had taken a short walk. None of this was possible the day before. I am convinced this type of recovery would not have been feasible without the increased prayers coming from Team Brausen.

Friday morning we saw our oncologist, Dr. Leach, who explained further the importance of Gary keeping to his current chemo schedule. He said, "Certain forms of cancer can become resistant to chemo and we do not want to give this cancer any opportunity it hasn't already taken. Gary, we chose this chemo schedule because you are strong, healthy, and young; though difficult you can handle the side effects…whatever they may be. If there is anything left of this cancer, it doesn't get to win."

Well, when you put it that way… So Gary is on for receiving another treatment Monday. His final chemo treatment will be July 17. They will rest his body for a month to six weeks, and then he will start a six-week, once-per-day radiation cycle at the point of where they removed his lung. Remember when our Doc told us he was aggressive? Well, he wasn't kidding.

Now, Team Brausen, if I may just love on you for a moment. I have no words that will justly describe either your outpouring of love upon my little family or our gratitude. Whether it be reading cancer books, doing our yard work, providing meals, supportive text messages, sending cards, saying full novenas, taking the boys on outings, walking with Gary, going on errands, keeping us laughing, or prayer, prayer, and more prayer, this victory is as much Gary's as it is yours. Your showering of love has been the fuel for which we fight each day with strength and perseverance that is not our own. Indeed, left to our own capacity, we would have never made it through the first doctor's appointment.

Each morning I awake, before I even open my eyes, I know that God is present in this circumstance—present through your prayers, present in His Word, and present in all your love, allowing us to get up each day and fight just a little harder than the day before.

Monday we start a new cycle, but amazingly within the last seventy-two hours we have been recharged and ready to go. (I am not sure Gary would use the verbiage "ready to go," but he is still sleeping and I have the keyboard.)

Entry 3: June 28, 2011—Three Weeks and a Day
(by Gary Brausen)

On June 6 I was administered my second treatment protocol out of four. A single treatment consists of several bags of intravenous fluids that include saline, potassium so my kidneys can process the harsh chemicals coursing through my body, antinausea medication that unfortunately wears off too soon, steroids, and of course the treatment drugs themselves. The process takes approximately six hours sitting in an airplane seat with approximately twenty others participating at the same time.

Going into this second session, the Brausens were ready. We had learned much from cycle number one and had prepared accordingly. We loaded coolers with cold clear fluids and stocked our shelves with bland, home cooking. Well, what happened in round two was nothing like what happened in round one. We were truly blindsided. In round one, I experienced mild nausea, extreme stomach cramping, and intense fatigue. Round two brought a bacterial sinus infection of biblical proportions that resulted in six consecutive sleepless nights spent coughing my brains out. I also experienced a stye cluster in my left eye that accumulated at least twelve styes on my upper left eyelid, causing extreme inflammation and pain that felt like wasps were continuously stinging my eye.

I remember trying to watch the final round of the U.S. Open at Congressional, and I absolutely had to turn it off because of the pain, even though I badly wanted to see Rory finish it off.

The bacterial infection came first and was thankfully treated fairly well with antibiotics, and the styes came later, leading to a three-week session with only three tolerable days of health.

Fatigue was also worse than the first time around and will probably get increasingly more difficult with each cycle. To give you an idea of the toll this has taken, Rosey and I walked a mile last Tuesday and it took nearly forty minutes. As I finally snapped out of this funk and reached a tolerable state, I walked four miles in just over an hour this past Sunday with a dear friend. Goes to show how quickly the body can recover from something like this.

This is why you have not heard from me for a while, which bums me out because I have a lot to say. The physical toll this time around was much more than I expected and took a severe toll on my emotional state. I suffered extreme irritability due partially to the chemicals coursing through my brain and the fact that I felt sicker than I had ever felt in my entire life. I have to say that it is very difficult to be pleasant with all of this going on. Emotionally, it got so difficult that I called my nurse last week and told her I was quitting. During an appointment last Thursday, Dr. Leach, who is my oncologist and unarguably one of the top doctors in the region, looked at me and said with his steely eyes, "I will have no part of you quitting. You will not quit, as this is our plan for success." When a guy with his reputation talks to you like that, you listen intently and you do what he says.

Spiritually, I had dark moments, which anyone can probably understand, and I am convinced that God fully understands as well. He knows what suffering can do to humans, knows specifically what I am dealing with, knows my challenges, and forgives me fully. My faith in Him and His Son are unshaken despite the hand I have been dealt.

That was the last three weeks. Let's talk about yesterday, which was the start of round three. Yesterday was a very emotional day for me for many reasons. The day started with a follow-up chest X-ray, which I was very concerned about after coughing so much over the last three weeks. If you remember, a cough is what started this entire surreal odyssey six months ago. Well, the chest X-ray was completely normal and my cough is just remnants of the bacterial infection suffered during round two.

I then asked to see if my surgeon was around on this day, as I had never officially thanked him for what he did for me. Seems a little weird thanking someone for removing a major organ, but he did save my life.

After asking his personal nurse, Lisa, if he was around, he was there in ten minutes. Here is one of the top thoracic surgeons in the region and he is taking time out of his day for me. This is the type of guy he is. He and I share a lot of things in common, including a love of the outdoors, the game of hockey, and golf. We are both handsome and intelligent. OK, the last one is a stretch. He is thirty-seven years old, is the most caring and talented physician I have ever met, and I believe is the only person who could have made this possible for me. When I saw him, I stood up, thanked him for saving my life, and we both wept. It was quite a moment indeed.

Rosey and I then chatted with Barb, an older woman, and her two daughters whom we had met during round one. If you look up the word *spunky* in the dictionary, her picture is right beside the definition. Rosey and I just hit it off so well with them and had a very lively chat to the point of possibly irritating some of the other patients. It was impossible to not have a lively and animated conversation with these three very special women. Barb later invited us to her home for some authentic Southern cooking later this year when we are both done with our treatments. What a celebration that will be.

Then another special lady came over for a chat. Her name is Sally, and I refer to her as the toughest and most positive person I know. She owns a hair salon in Burnsville and has missed only three days of work since January of this year, despite continuous, aggressive treatment regimens. She continues to cut hair and run her salon effectively but cannot feel her hands or toes. I admire Sally so much in so many ways and she is just a joy to talk to.

Then I noticed something different about the "room" yesterday. I noticed at least four young men in their twenties being administered day-long treatments. All four looked to be in good health, except for one, and I wondered what their stories are. I am hoping to see them again in three weeks when I undergo my fourth and final treatment. It reaffirmed in my mind that this disease has no boundaries or conscience. I write this to you all on day one of treatment three, typically a good day because I am hyped up on steroids and the antinausea medication is still at work.

I am apprehensive as to what is going to come in the upcoming days, but I am not afraid. I know this is part of the plan for success and a huge part of the permanent solution. Please continue to pray hard for minimal side effects and a full and long-lasting recovery from this insidious disease for me.

Blessings to all of Team Brausen.

Entry 4: July 4—All in a Day

Today, Gary started his day at 6:00 a.m. He headed to Jerry's Grocery Store. He had a craving, but he wasn't sure for what. He left the store with breakfast sausage, bananas, a pack of gum, and frozen White Castle burgers. He came home but didn't want to wake me, and nothing he bought sounded good, so he left again—this time the destination was McDonald's for their big breakfast.

All this running around made him tired—a nap was sounding really good. He woke up at 10:00 a.m. nauseated, so he had a bowl of watermelon. He was enjoying another energy spurt, so we headed out to Home Depot. The errand was short because his energy depleted quickly. The nausea was returning, and pizza rolls and cherries sounded good. He rested for a bit.

His dad stopped by for a visit. They watched some of the ball game. Being hungry again, this time chicken noodle soup hit the spot. Shortly after his dad left, nausea returned, and the White Castle burgers helped. We took a short walk when he was done.

After our walk and a little more rest, nausea made another attempt. He had a hamburger, celery, radishes, and carrots for dinner. A little bit after dinner, he enjoyed a nice burst of energy, so we went for our first bike ride since his diagnosis. We rode very slowly for five and a half miles. I know this because not even cancer can beat the geek out of an engineer (sorry, Seagate friends, but I know you are smiling…just a little.) He tracked our whole bike ride on his phone—elevations, miles, pace per mile, and more. I teased him a little, but in truth I had to ride slightly ahead of him so he wouldn't see me cry. I was so happy with the little return of normalcy. Plus, I love the geeky side of Gary. He thinks I also need this app on my phone. I just smiled; he doesn't remember that I don't even call my voicemail.

As much as the nausea cycled today, so did his emotions. He was joyful that the boys had returned after a weekend with their aunt Donna, frustrated at his body's weaknesses and that the light bulb he needed was difficult to find at Home Depot, grateful that the fatigue had lifted some and that he could go on a simple errand, angry that he would be missing fireworks with the boys, happy that the White Castle burgers tasted good, disappointed that he was missing the celebrations of such a great holiday weekend, envious that others were not, and excited that his phone could track our whole bike ride, trail and all. These emotions were as intense as they were varied.

As I write this, he is up again with nausea—the White Castle burgers don't sound good, but maybe a Popsicle will do. None of this was possible yesterday (except the cravings). He slept most of the day.

Tomorrow, who knows? My little sister Donna sent me a great line about hope. She wrote, "Just remember the day before they discovered penicillin there was no penicillin." So true…what a difference one day can make.

Does this sound insane? That's because it was. Yet God continued to be faithful. He touched our family with such profound kindness.

DIRTY WINDOWS AND THE GOODNESS OF GOD

After a particularly difficult night, Gary was lying on the couch in the kitchen finally resting. The kids were still sleeping and I was at my desk trying to make sense of the mounting medical paperwork. It was about 7:30 a.m. and the sun was hitting our windows at just the right angle to show the winter, spring, and summer layers of dirt that had accumulated on them. Somehow those dirty windows were like a knockout punch to my resolve.

Granted, I was overtired and the fallout from Gary's most recent chemo was brutal, so my excuses were many, but I just couldn't let go of that cloudy dirt. Even when Gary was healthy, cleaning the windows had always been one of my jobs. I wasn't the one who was sick. I should still have been able to get to them, yet they had become such a low priority. Somehow, at that moment, in my fatigued mind, they represented everything I felt cancer was stealing from me: my husband's health, his mental state, our financial security, and stability for my children. I felt my Irish temper flair up; cancer was not going to take my windows too.

Gary was moaning in his sleep, and it was apparent to me that it was not going to be a day I could clean windows, or anything else for that matter. My next thought was that if I couldn't get to them myself, then I must have a coupon for window cleaning somewhere; I could pay to have them done just this once, or I could ask Team Brausen.

As I searched for a coupon, Gary's pain was calling me back to reality. Finding a coupon was a futile effort. I wasn't going to spend $180 on window cleaning when we were living on disability and my husband was battling cancer, and though Team Brausen was more than willing, I was feeling quite indebted for all they were already doing for us. No, cleaning the windows would have to wait.

The resignation in my spirit was oddly peaceful. Somewhere in my mind I knew that it really wasn't about clean windows. It had everything to do with the by-product of cancer in my own life. Cancer had robbed me of the delusion that I was in control.

I looked up to the Lord and said, "The windows too? You want me to give up the clean windows too?" I let out a resigned sigh, paused a minute, and in complete submission I gave up to the Lord the importance of having clean windows. I helped Gary through a tough episode, and then I went back to my paperwork in complete peace.

About an hour and half later, there was a knock on the door. When I opened the door, a very unassuming man was there with a notepad in his hands. He introduced himself as Nate, and then he proceeded to tell me he was a window cleaner. As I was making polite conversation with Nate, internally I was thinking about how much I hated Satan.

Nate told me he had just cleaned the windows of my neighbors down the street. We exchanged a few more Midwestern pleasantries, then Nate asked me if he could schedule a time to do my windows. I looked at him and somehow mustered a smile, though calling it sincere would be a stretch. I politely told him, "No, thank you."

He looked at me dumbfounded and said, "You don't want the gift?"

"What gift?" I asked.

"Well, your neighbors, Rita and Bob, down the street just paid to have your windows cleaned."

I stammered and stuttered some kind of thank you. I set up an appointment, closed the door, and sat down on my staircase and just cried. God is so good and generous. Who was I to have such favor? I was no one special, just a normal person like everyone else. But to God I am His love, His creation, His daughter, and in His lavish style He just wanted to let me know He was still on His throne, caring about every little detail of our lives. The truth is that He feels exactly the same about you too!

Cancer had brought me to the most vulnerable, broken state and God used my brokenness to remind me that we are solely and completely reliant on the most amazing, providing, merciful God for everything—even clean windows. Cancer robbed me of delusion and ignorance, but God filled me back up with the truth.

The best part was that when we told Rita and Bob how their

generosity had impacted our journey, they were delighted and loved that they had been obedient to a prompt God had placed in their hearts. You just can't make that kind of stuff up.

GOING TO LONDON

Another amazing miracle in our journey was our trip to London after Gary's fourth and final chemo treatment. Gary was in the process of passing through hopefully the worst of the fourth treatment. Each of the four treatments brought to Gary very unique side effects and each cycle was taking a greater toll on him physically, mentally, and emotionally. The doctors warned us that the effects and intensity of this chemo regimen would be cumulative, but we were never quite prepared for what was to come. Nausea and fatigue were his constant companions for the previous week, but Saturday night brought on something entirely different. Around 11:00 p.m. Gary began to suffer neck, back, and chest spasms that left him in excruciating pain.

This pain persisted through Tuesday, finally lifting some on Wednesday and Thursday. If you haven't figured it out by now, Gary can be tough and more than slightly stubborn. He would only take pain meds for about twenty-four hours because he didn't want that "stuff" in his system. As much as he can drive me crazy, he was so determined and has such heart.

During this episode, my sister MJ and I were discussing all the different levels of burden people are currently carrying. Some of these burdens are short-lived, while others will be carried for a lifetime. We discussed the despair that could easily be ours if we did not live a life of faith.

Our conversation reminded me of something I read some time ago about the type of faith that pleases God. Faith that pleases God is earnest, seeking, and believing as real fact what is not revealed to the senses. He delights in the fact that we believe even though we cannot see. The more we walk in the expectation of His loving character, the more we open ourselves up to receive the overflowing of His love. The clincher here, of course, is that we cannot control, dictate, or persuade His love—we can only receive it. Yeah, this last part can be difficult—we have no control. In truth, the first part can be a journey too.

This happened to be my circumstances the previous week. You see, ten days prior to Gary's diagnosis we booked tickets to visit my sister in London on July 30. The tickets were beyond our budget, but I felt the Lord directing us to make the reservations and trust Him. I even heard a dollar figure at which to purchase the tickets. On March 1, for about twenty-four hours, the ticket price dropped $500, to within $60 of the original figure I had heard, so I purchased. I wasn't going to get legalistic about $60.

When our life turned upside down ten days later, a trip to London seemed like an impossibility, especially when we realized the fourth treatment was only two weeks before departure. So in order to give Gary as much time as possible to recover and keep to our radiation schedule, we asked the airline to adjust the tickets by two weeks. The price for this request was another $3,800. The rest of the story makes me chuckle.

I wish I could tell it to you without looking ridiculous,

but this is an impossibility. But I will tell the story anyway, because by the end you will see God's glory, His patience, and His love wrapped all around my humanness.

I was completely convinced that God wanted Gary to have this trip without having to pay $3,800. So I went about executing my plan. In truth, calling it a "plan" is a slight exaggeration—it was more like a persistent approach. First, I asked our doctor for a note, which waived the change-of-ticket fees, but we were still saddled with the change-of-fare fees of $2,800. So for about a month I asked everyone I came into contact with if they knew of anyone within the airline who had the authority to waive the remaining fees. Thanks to loving friends and family, I received many names but no one could help make this happen.

My next attempt was very scientific: I started calling the airline customer service line, praying for a person capable of changing our situation. If the customer service rep didn't seem helpful, I would hang up. This went on for about two weeks. I was getting nowhere. If you are thinking, "With that approach, no wonder," you can now appreciate my humility in sharing this story.

The break finally came, however. While Gary was sleeping, and the boys were at a friend's house, God moved in my spirit. I heard, "Tonight you will get your tickets." Obediently, I called the airline and started working with a very "not so nice" representative. Well, typically I would have hung up and try again, but I was trusting God. I worked with this individual for about forty-five minutes, and though try as she might, she could only lower the ticket price another $100. But then a funny thing happened. All of a sudden her computer crashed and she had to transfer me to another agent. Thank goodness we were not on Skype because I don't think she would have appreciated my Irish jig of celebration. My sails were full—I was ready to see God work His miracle.

The next agent was like working with an angel. She reentered our story and worked for about an hour to get the fee down to $355 per ticket. I was overjoyed at her diligence but knew that this was still not good enough. Finally, I asked her what she thought we should do. She simply said, "I would trust and wait until July 29, the fairs could still come down, or at that time we could make a decision to take a travel credit." I heard wisdom and conceded the fight for the evening.

In pure disbelief I closed down my computer. I just couldn't believe I didn't have those tickets, and I couldn't believe I was wrong in my spirit or that I heard the Lord's leading wrong. Frankly, I asked God if this was a lesson in pride. Did I need to ask for help in covering the additional cost of the trip? No, He had me lay down my pride on about day five of Gary's diagnosis—so that wasn't it. I asked again, "Lord, did I leave a rock unturned?" I ran down every lead I was given. Well, then what was it?

Gently, He brought to memory a story my sister MJ had conveyed about the apostles and Jesus. When Jesus had come to the apostles after the crucifixion, He told them He would visit them again, but He did not tell them when or where. What did the apostles do? They just continued on with life. They returned to their jobs and went fishing. Then one dawn, after a particularly unlucky night of doing everything in their power to catch fish, they saw Jesus on shore and He told them where to cast their nets. They did as He told them and they brought their nets up full of fish.

As I recalled this story, I heard God say, "Rosey, ask Me where to cast your net."

Humbly, and a little ridiculously, I said, "Lord, I have done everything in my power to get us to London. Where do You want me to cast my net?"

"Chicago," was His response.

"Really?" I asked. Waiting for the computer to reboot felt like an eternity. Silent tears fell down my cheeks. There it was—a flight for the exact fee that I had originally bought our tickets. I quickly called the airline and verified that we could get on that flight. Of course, they said yes and all we had to incur was $20 per ticket for the change-of-airport fee.

We drove to Chicago on August 9, stayed with my brother Frank and his wife, Pam, for the night, and left the next day for London. Pam is a cancer survivor herself and had assisted Gary through this whole process. Gary had wanted to give her one big "Gary hug" for the longest time. He was still apprehensive as to his travel readiness, but as far as he was concerned, this detour was all part of God's plan.

We made it to London via Chicago, and God faithfully used the time to restore our family, and, most importantly, the trip helped Gary to feel empowered. He had lost so much of himself over the last few months. Hugging my brother Frank and his wife, Pam, filled Gary immensely. Just the normalcy of having dinner in their home after a long drive was its own tonic.

Navigating an overseas trip for someone in perfect health is exhausting; managing it while fighting cancer is outrageous. Yet Gary was triumphant. From the overabundant generosity of my sister Kathy and brother-in-law Kemper, to the change of scenery, to the wonderful hospitality of the United Kingdom, the trip was just what we needed to get ready for the final portion of our journey—radiation.

Gary, Alec, Rosey, and Bennett in London two weeks after Gary's fourth chemo treatment.

Chapter 8

Radiation and the Enemy

The man that guards the gate opens the gate for the shepherd. And the sheep listen to the voice of the shepherd. The shepherd calls his own sheep, using their names, and he leads them out. The shepherd brings all of his sheep out. Then he goes ahead of them and leads them. The sheep follow him because they know his voice (John 10:34 ERV).

Upon returning from London, we went into full back-to-school mode. My job was gearing up, the kids needed school supplies, and Gary was getting ready to start radiation.

After Gary was fitted for his chest harness, we met with his radiation oncologist Laura Willson, who was very kind and direct, which we had come to expect from Gary's medical team. She went through the plan with us: Gary would need six and a half weeks of radiation because the margins were positive at the site of his pneumomectomy (lung removal), meaning they still knew that cancer was left behind. She was clear with us that radiation was not a cure for cancer but an opportunity to give it a knockdown blow. Gary's cancer was aggressive and she was hoping that radiation would buy him more time.

We sat and listened to the horrible side effects for Gary's procedure—horrible because the esophagus was in the direct path of the radiation, so it was going to take an awful hit. We discussed potential need of feeding tubes, the pain of coughing, and on and on it went. We listened to the percentage of possibility that Gary could encounter these side effects, as well as the plan for administering the radiation if the side effects occurred. We both listened to what was being said. Gary nodded his head, asked questions, and was completely calm. I, on the other hand, was sick to my stomach.

We drove home and discussed our plan with my work schedule, as well as everything else we had going on. We decided that Gary's dad would stay with him most of the time and help him through the process. We talked about how well the boys were doing and how we could help them through this next phase as well. Even though we talked about a lot of things, we didn't talk about the doctor's appointment.

Somehow, in the months following Gary's diagnosis, I had become comfortable with Gary's denial. In truth, however, it helped me compartmentalize my own feelings because at this point in our journey not talking about the future seemed fairly normal.

When we pulled into the driveway that day, Gary's good friend Scott was waiting for us and a promised bike ride with Gary. After such an awful meeting, I was hoping that Gary would have sat with his friend and discussed at least a little of what he was going to be going through or feeling. But what I witnessed made me feel like I was in another dimension altogether.

Apparently Gary had never discussed needing radiation with Scott, and since Scott wasn't a daily CaringBridge reader, he was completely clueless as to the next phase of Gary's journey. Scott was so in the dark that I felt bad for him. Later that night, I drove over to his house to fill him in on what was really happening. I felt like if Gary came into any sort of awareness, he would need Scott to stand with him.

After Scott went home, Gary came up to me and gave me a big hug. He looked at me, and said, "Rosey, now why do I need radiation? The cancer is gone, right?"

I should have received an Academy Award for my performance. "Absolutely, Gary. It's gone. They just want to make sure to get any wayward cells that may be hanging around."

"Good. That is what I thought," he said.

"Gary, did our meeting with Laura scare you?" I asked hesitantly.

"No, she didn't really say anything important."

"OK, good," I said.

The depths of his denial were so freaky but so strangely amazing, it was as if he wasn't even in the meeting. To date, Gary has very little recall of this appointment with the radiation oncologist, and because of his lack of recall I adjusted the details of our CaringBridge site. It was becoming increasingly difficult to keep the worlds of denial and reality separate. And this troubled me greatly.

The next morning, as I was in that delicious suspended space right before you wake up, I heard the Lord say, "You need the prayer of My will."

"Oh, Lord, what prayer is that?" I asked. "You know I am not good at memorizing—I don't know a prayer of Your will."

"You know it, sweet child. Our Father—"

"Oh yes, Lord, 'Our Father who art in heaven, hallowed be Thy name. Thy kingdom come, Thy *will* be done, on earth as it is done in heaven.'" I woke up saying the Our Father and my spirit soared.

As it turns out, Gary did not suffer one of the horrendous side effects that were predicted. His skin became a little sore but nothing compared to what I was prepared for. He did have bursitis act up in his shoulder, which sent him through the roof in pain, especially when they would put him in the correct position for radiation. The pain was so intense he would weep. However, we knew that was nothing compared to what could have been. Not only was Gary spared horrible side effects of radiation, but God was also busy in His God way, bringing healing to Gary in a whole different sector of his life—his relationship with his father.

When Gary was a boy, his dad, Donovan (Heni), suffered from severe depression. Gary was just ten years old when Heni was hospitalized for the first time. As you might imagine, this was a very hard and difficult time in Heni's life, as in the '70s there was precious little understanding about chronic depression. At home his mom, Shirley, did an excellent job of keeping everything going. She worked to keep meals on the table and to be both mom and dad to the boys, but she, like me, could not completely shield her sons from what they were encountering.

Gary remembers very little from this period of his life, only that he started to wash his hands repeatedly before bed, imagined creatures in his bed as he tried to sleep, and recalls never feeling safe. When Heni returned, he wasn't in the best emotional state, which had many manifestations. Needless to say, Gary carried around many wounds from this period of his childhood. He didn't necessarily understand that his dad's behavior was due to depression—what child would?

During the course of Gary's radiation treatments, his dad never left his side. Radiation sent Gary into the deepest places of fatigue. He would be awake for only small increments of time throughout the day and then be back to sleep again. If Gary slept, then Heni would doze off too. If Gary wanted to take a small walk, Heni would be right by his side. This time with his dad was an unexpected healing that still bears fruit to this day.[6]

As Gary finished up his radiation in late October of 2011, he was eager to get back into the throws of life. He desperately wanted to get back to work—as insecure as he was in his ability to keep up after all he had missed, his desire to "get back at it" was stronger. For myself, I questioned whether or not this was wise. My preference would have been for him to spend more

---

6 Heni still suffers from depression, but he is amazing in how he uses behavior modifications to live his life. He doesn't hide when he is in a bout of depression; in fact, he does the exact opposite. When invited to come over to our house, he often says he is in the crapper (which means depression for him), but he'll come over anyway. Heni is one of my favorite people in this world—I just love his heart.

time in recovery, but I also knew that if he didn't get back to work we could soon be facing depression as well as anxiety. It was my dad who helped me understand Gary's drive and gave me the motivation to support him in his decision.

My dad had told me that while he was recovering from a near-death MS attack in 1966, the only thing he wanted to do was to get well to provide for his then seven children. It was his sole desire to fulfill this role, and it is what pushed and motivated him to get well. He further explained that I may never understand this impulse, but I could show my love for Gary and faith in him by supporting his decision. When imparting his wisdom, he didn't neglect to raise his eyebrow and look over his reading glasses at me. Even at forty-five years old, that glance still could work its magic like I was seven years old again. I think I might have even responded, "Yes, sir."

Gary started work again very slowly in mid-November, half days at first, then just a little bit more. The compassion of his Seagate coworkers, boss, and upper management are a textbook example of how the spirit of a company lies within the heart of its employees. They were amazingly patient and compassionate toward Gary and our whole family—truly wonderful people.

One of the hundreds of examples of their encouragement came as Gary was walking into the building on his first day back to work after being gone almost nine months. As he approached the building from the parking lot, he heard clapping behind him. It was his coworker Kent applauding his return. When he came home that night, he told me it was this gesture, along with countless others, that made him feel like one day he would be back to his old self.

Gary did return to work, but he was still fighting cancer plus the side effects of chemotherapy and radiation. For the better part of the next three years, he would wake up each morning nauseous, weak, and wobbly. It would take him one and a half to two hours every morning before he felt good, so he would get up at 5:30 or 6:00 a.m. every day to get to work by 8:00 or 8:30 a.m. This was a great change for a man whose morning routine used to consist of a fifteen-minute bathroom drill, shovel down breakfast, and run out the door in thirty minutes from start to finish.

The evenings were no better. Typically after work, Gary would bike for at least forty-five minutes and lift some light weights at Seagate's gym before heading home. During those days, when he came home proud for his daily accomplishments, I often had to hold my tongue. He looked gaunt, fatigued, and his skin still had a yellowish tint to it; I was not above lying to him, telling him he looked just the opposite. Instead, I prayed for ways I could support him without taking away his drive. I would assert a gentle word of caution about pushing it too hard here and there, but after a while I stopped trying—Gary was fighting his way, and words of caution from me or anyone else were falling on deaf ears.

When he would get home, his evening routine was the same: he would eat dinner, take a nap, and then go to bed by 9:30 p.m. It's hard to explain how the boys and I felt about this new Gary. In our minds we knew he was back at work providing for our family and we were ecstatically thankful that his emotions had started to level out, but we missed him.

While he was going through treatment, we had all quickly become accustomed to a present and engaged husband and father, even though his circumstances were difficult. Gary felt isolated from us as well. He was angry with his body for taking so long to recover, wishing that he could stay up and watch a movie with us or muster enough energy to go on an outing. It was a mixed bag of gratitude and change. We were quickly learning that recovery was going to be a bit messy.

After a particularly difficult Saturday of strained tempers and stretched expectations, Bennett met me in the kitchen. "Mom," he said, "Dad is well but he's not the same Dad that he used to be."

"I know, honey," I responded. "I'm afraid it's going to take some time. What things are you missing about him?"

"It's really hard to explain, Mom. He is fighting so hard, and I can see that every day; it's just that he used to go outside in the middle of winter wearing only a down vest. Do you remember how you would get after him for not dressing warmer?"

I had to chuckle at this memory because it had been a point of contention with Gary and me for years. I was trying to teach Bennett and Alec how to dress warm for the elements—you know, keep your mittens on, wear a coat and hat—and then Gary would walk around outdoors wearing barely anything at all, proclaiming that Minnesotans are built tough. Since they are boys, of course they followed the example of their dad. This used to rev my engines.

"Yes, Bennett, I remember," I responded.

"Well, now it's like he lost that part of himself. He is always so bundled up and afraid of getting cold. He doesn't stay up late with us anymore; he won't sit by a campfire. He doesn't do a lot of dad things—am I horrible for wishing that I could get my old dad back, the dad who was tough and rugged and didn't worry about every little thing?"

"No, you're not horrible for missing that part of Dad. We have to be patient, Bennett. He is trying so hard and it is going to take a while. Plus, that rugged part of Dad you are looking for is right before your eyes; it's just manifested in a different way."

"I know, Mom. That is why I feel so bad for saying anything. I should feel like the luckiest kid around, but I am still wishing for more."

"Bennett, I'm just happy you are being honest. We all wish for more. It's hard to walk in complete gratitude every moment when you have lost a part of your dad that you loved. Even though we are blessed beyond measure, we still have to mourn the change. God is so patient with us, Bennett. You never have to feel bad for being honest. I'm not disappointed in you, and neither is God."

"So it's OK?" he asked.

"Yes, B, it's OK."

"Do you think he will ever be that same dad again?" he asked tentatively.

"I don't know, honey, because I'm not sure what the 'same old dad' really represents anymore. Let me put it this way: do you think you are ever going to be able to go back to that kid you were before Dad got sick?"

"No, I guess not," he said. "I see things with so much more compassion now, and I feel like I'm more aware of how things are pretty fragile."

"Yes, plus, whether you know it or not, you are a much stronger person now than you were before. God uses each experience that we go through to build us into better people. So no, I don't think Dad is going to be the same as he used to be. I think he is going to be much better, much more compassionate and aware of the suffering of others. This will change how he reacts in his day-to-day life too. Actually, he might learn that I was right after all, and he does need to wear a coat in winter."

I had to laugh at my own cleverness. Bennett gave me a sly smile.

"Bennett, I also think he will return to his old self as well," I reassured him. "You can't kill the cocky in Daddy. Mark my words: one day I'm going to be after him for some other 'Minnesota tough' ideal he has, and life will feel normal if not just a wee bit adjusted."

Bennett's frankness opened up an area in my own heart. I missed my funny, sophomoric, irreverent husband more than I had allowed myself to admit. I brought this to the Lord's feet, laid it down, and didn't wait for an answer. I knew God heard my heart. I also knew we had to walk out this trial.

GARY IS PRAYED FOR A THIRD TIME

God's timing is always perfect, and He chose this time in our journey to have a group of people gather at our house to lay hands on Gary and our friend John (Mic) Michelau. The

Allisons, Russells, Mary, and Kathy, who was Mic's wife, all came to pray over Gary and Mic. It was a wonderful afternoon full of worship and praise. God brought to mind the Scripture from James 5:14: "Is anyone among you sick? Then he must call for the elders of the church and they are to pray over him, anointing him with oil in the name of the Lord."

In my relationship with God, I find Him to be a lot less legalistic than we are in our human state on many topics. Long ago He worked with me on my definition of church. First, He stretched me to look beyond it being a four-walled structure, then He challenged my understanding of what a denomination is, and then He took me on a journey that was amazingly radical for me.

He taught me to consider what it means to have the Holy Spirit, the Spirit of the great I AM housed and residing within my body. He taught me that since the Holy Spirit dwelt within me, then "church" was happening a lot more often than I thought. Church was taking place any time I was discussing, worshiping, praying, encouraging, and edifying another Christian. If this is the case, I actually spend a lot of time in "church."

This took me a while to understand, but I started to watch what would happen when two or more were gathered in His name. Beautiful things happened. Acts of service were completed, people were prayed for and encouraged, and we grew in wisdom and knowledge through shared life experiences. It is so like God's nature not to want to wait for Sundays to be in relationship with His beloved and move His kingdom forward.

This does not mean that I am dismissing the authority or benefit of our formal churches. It is extremely important to be part of a community of believers under a person trained in the Word and given the gift of ministry. However, I am saying our idea or ideals of church could use some expanding. Since God had already stretched me in this area when this Scripture came to mind, I had no problem understanding or believing its significance for our prayer meeting.

The place where I work, Bethany Academy, is a K–12 Christian school, not a church. However, it is a community of believers, and everyone present that afternoon was tied to it in some fashion. If Bethany were to have an elder in the traditional sense, it would be Mike Allison, so I gave Mike anointing oil from Israel, and he blessed and prayed over both Gary and Mic.

Gary kneeled down at Mike's feet. As Mike prayed over him, I saw in my husband's eyes the pureness of complete faith. I have only witnessed such faith two other times in my life. Gary was completely and wholly willing to receive the miracle of healing from the Lord. His eyes did not reflect a fear of unworthiness, there was no what-if scenarios running through his mind, and there was absolutely no question to his belief that God's will was to heal him.

Our dear friend Mic's eyes were closed, so I didn't get to witness what was taking place in his heart. Mic was being prayed for because three years earlier he began suffering from a very aggressive form of Parkinson's disease. He had been a beloved teacher at Bethany Academy for thirty-five years. Parkinson's robbed this world of an amazing man of God as well as a great teacher.

Mic did not receive physical healing that afternoon that we could qualify, but his wife, Kathy, received emotional and spiritual healing. Later she would tell me that after that prayer meeting God had met her in her heart and that she was able to cherish the moments she still had remaining with Mic. (Mic went home to be with the Lord on March 3, 2013.)

We ended the prayer meeting with communion. Mike reminded us of two Scriptures, the first of which was prophesied two thousand years before Christ came, and the second was written after Jesus's death and resurrection:

> But He was pierced through for our transgressions, He was crushed for our iniquities; the chastening for our well-being fell upon Him, and by His scourging we are healed (Isaiah 53:5).

And the second one was:

> And He Himself bore our sins in His body on the cross, so that we might die to sins and live for righteousness; for by His wounds you were healed (1 Peter 2:24).

In both Greek and Hebrew, the word *healed* can mean either physical or spiritual healing. I was praying that for Gary and Mic it meant both.

THE ENEMY WILL STOP AT NOTHING TO BREAK YOUR RESOLVE

Throughout the whole process, Gary and the boys each fought their way through fear and anxiety. It took on different forms, but in the end it always had the same root. I am truly in awe of how they battled. They were each steadfast in the truth and courageously worked with behavior modifications to hold back the tides of the worry, fear, and anxiety that would come. I watched them each grow so much during those months. I have come to realize that the very trials that broke my heart for each of them are the very character traits that now make me beam with pride. They have each become much stronger men for the world.

My battle, however, was completely and wholly different than theirs. Satan would attack with all sorts of manipulations to deplete my resolve. A friend trying to "help" me accept Gary's diagnosis, fatigue to such a degree that I couldn't think straight, on and on they went. But the worst attack came as Gary went back to work and the date of his next CT scan was quickly approaching. If all calculations were correct, the doctors expected to see cancer in one of Gary's vital organs in February of 2012.

In late December of 2011, I began to hear a different message. The voice was tender and loving, like the voice of God, but something just wasn't right: "Rosey, you have done a great job fighting. I love your spirit and your heart, but now I need you to help Gary out of denial. The healing I am giving you is time. My ultimate wish is to bring him home."

The first time I heard this I wept and wept. "No! Lord! Your will is to heal! It's all over Scripture! I am standing! You are a God who fulfills His promise! You are the very God who brought those Scriptures to my mind!" I was a two-year-old throwing a tantrum.

The voice was quiet for a few days. Then it would return: "Rosey, sweet child, you need to be the one to tell Gary. It's only fair. At this point you are now lying to him. Don't worry; I will give you the courage and strength."

"But, Lord, there are so many biblical examples of how You have changed Your mind when the faithful stood. Remember Abraham's plea for Lot, or the persistent widow before the judge. Lord, I am asking You to spare Gary," I pleaded.

The voice left again, but only for a few days. And then it would return again—always kind and always loving. But as the time for his next appointment grew closer, it came with more and more intensity, reminding me that I was running out of time.

It broke me to such a point that even writing this chapter makes me shudder. I didn't tell anyone about my dilemma. I kept it solely to myself. I wept at the burden in private, often taking drives to cry or closing the bathroom door to sob into a towel to muffle the sound. My mental state was in shambles. How I worked, took care of the kids, and reinforced Gary all at the same time was pure example of God's grace and strength.

The worst part was that during this time I had stopped seeking God. Think about it: if you know you are willfully being disobedient to God, you really don't want to be in His presence. It was a stark and desolate place to be. It was far worse than any place I could have ever imagined, a place of no hope, no comfort, complete and utter loneliness and despair.

As the appointment was drawing near, the voice grew in frequency and the words and reasoning became craftier. The burden was nonstop. I just couldn't do what I thought God was asking of me. I wasn't strong enough to do it. Not only that, but there was something that didn't sit right in my spirit. For these reasons and many more, I remained silent.

I felt like Jonah in the Bible, who didn't want to talk to the Ninevites, and who instead ran from God. The only thing missing was the whale. Yet I knew I was weakening. Who was I to go against God's plan? Didn't I trust Him explicitly, even with my husband's life? Hadn't I promised Him early on that I would be obedient no matter what and that He would always be my God?

Sometime during the summer of 2011, during Gary's chemo treatments, I had sought out the help of a Christian counselor for the boys and myself. I was well beyond my scope of knowledge on how to parent children through a potentially terminal illness; we all needed a place to be real in all the confusion and pain of watching Gary suffer.

Our counselor's name was Rhonda. The boys went four times and then they were done—they didn't like it at all. I guess it was me who was the one in need, because I kept going. I shared every part of myself, my marriage, and Gary's journey with Rhonda, but I didn't tell her about the voice I was hearing or my disobedience. I held it even from her, until the night before Gary's appointment.

It was the eve of my ultimate betrayal, and I was no longer able to compartmentalize my mental state. I came completely unglued in my chair. She listened, gave me Kleenex, gave me more Kleenex, and finally she just gave me the box. She listened and listened as I poured out my soul to her.

When she spoke, she simply said, "Rosey, rarely do I get to

witness a faith so transparent. You are under attack. This isn't the voice of God. It is an imposter. You are not lying to Gary."

I looked at her blankly. "I'm under attack?" I asked. "But the voice sounds just like God's?"

She reminded me of the craftiness of Satan and 2 Corinthians 11:14: "No wonder, for even Satan disguises himself as an angel of light." She affirmed that I could not be obedient to the voice I was hearing because the message wasn't consistent to who I knew God to be. This was not His nature.

I sat up straighter. "I'm not being disobedient?" I asked.

"No. Tomorrow will be what tomorrow is."

I cannot explain the weight that lifted off my shoulders that day. All of a sudden I was so light, so free. How could I not have known it wasn't God? How could I not have known I was under attack? I was completely flabbergasted.

She went onto say, "Rosey, God has kept the truth from Gary out of His goodness. Based on Gary's mental state prior to surgery, do you think he could have fought as strongly if he was entertaining his potential death? Do you think he could have really kept his eyes on the Lord?"

I had to agree with Rhonda here. Based on Gary's level of anxiety through the process, it would have been very difficult for him to keep his eyes fixed on the Lord.

"Rosey, didn't God tell you before there was even a diagnosis that Gary would need to 'walk in his healing' and lean on you?" she asked.

"Yes," I said. "So how could Gary successfully walk in his healing if he feared death? Is that what you mean?"

"Yes. Gary's denial, for where he is on his spiritual journey, has been a gift. Remember, God is nothing if not consistent. He would not have you be the person to take back the gift. He would have worked that out with Gary himself. It is God's job to prepare our hearts for all of life's circumstances…and if He did have you help, you would have peace and courage in your spirit. He would have prepared your heart too."

My spirit heard wisdom that day. I wept new tears. Had I listened to that horrible voice, I would have stripped Gary of the denial he needed to continue the fight, and I knew we were still a long way from victory.

That night Satan tried one more time to convince me to confront Gary. "Rosey, Rhonda is a wonderful counselor, but you know my voice—" I stopped in my tracks and cut the voice off by quoting Scripture out loud. I told Satan to get behind me, Gary and I would walk into victory together, and tomorrow would bring what tomorrow brings.

The next morning Gary and I were both in a very pensive state—it was a big day. As we were backing out of our driveway, I heard, "This is your last chance. Tell him now." I mentally flipped Satan the bird.

A block later, a huge eagle swooped down in front of our car. I couldn't believe it. Silent tears rolled down my cheeks. I took Gary's hand and told him that I was sure that the test results would be clear. He looked at me, but I could tell he was still stunned by the eagle.

"Rosey, haven't you always told me that eagles remind you of God?" he asked.

"Yep, they are mentioned all the time in the Bible." Then I quoted Isaiah 40:31: "But those who hope in the LORD will renew their strength. They will soar on wings like eagles; they will run and not grow weary, they will walk and not be faint" (NIV).

"Well, that was amazing! That had to be sent from God," he said. But then he quickly added, "I'm still so scared though."

"I know, Gary. I'm scared too, but let's keep our eyes on God. OK?"

Gary got out his *God's Promises* book, and we recited Scripture all the way to the hospital. Was the feeling in my stomach butterflies or knots? It was impossible to tell.

When we arrived at the oncology office, it seemed like it took forever to get through the process of being checked-in. First, they needed to draw blood. Then we had to wait to be called into a room to see Gary's oncologist. Before we got to see the oncologist, however, a nurse's aid came and took Gary's vitals, followed by the oncology nurse who discussed medications and concerns or changes from last visit. Finally, it was time for the oncologist. This usually only takes about fifteen minutes from start to finish, but this day it felt like hours.

Dr. Leach entered the room and without any banter or niceties he said, "It's all clear!" He is so sensitive to the journey of his patients. He told us that he had realized long ago from his own experience that patients just want to hear the test results. They don't care about what comes next until the results are given.[7]

---

7   We couldn't have asked for a more experienced, personable, kind, approachable, and "Rocky Balboa" type of doctor. To this day I continue to pray for him. He has such a privileged position in this world. He walks with those fighting the worst of circumstances. He lives on the very edge with each and every one of them, yet he makes an individual feel like they are his only concern.

Gary wept and I took a deep breath. I had been crying for the past two months. I didn't have a tear left that day. We had made it through the first hurdle. There would be three more CT scans and eighteen months before I could tell Gary the truth about his diagnosis, eighteen more months before we had medical proof of what I already knew in my spirit. But that was an unbelievably good day.

Gary and Greg,
Shirley, Chris, and Heni.
Three weeks after surgery.

Chapter 9

Why Isn't
Everyone Healed?

In the beginning of April of 2012, Alec was feeling pretty down. His friends had been extremely supportive during the whole cancer process, but he would get frustrated at times. Even though his friends were extremely kind, no one really understood how difficult life had become for him. He told me one night, "Mom, I love my friends, but I just wish I knew someone who understood what it's like having a dad fighting cancer."

"I know, honey," I said. "I understand, and so does your brother. Can that be enough?"

"Sure, I guess," was his response, but he wasn't convinced. I have since learned of many organizations that serve this exact purpose, but at the time I was clueless.

JULIE, KEN, AND SAM HULL

Three weeks later, Bethany's admissions director, Kelli, was giving a new family a tour of the school. As a family they were very happy, yet the color of the father's skin looked way too familiar: was he naturally bald or was that from cancer?

A few weeks after their tour they decided to send Sam to

Bethany. Kelli came into my office and told me their story. She was tentative about involving me, but she just couldn't look past the coincidences. She asked if I would give Julie, the mom, a call.

With more than a little trepidation, I called Julie. I get it; cancer is the great equalizer, right? I didn't feel like I had much to give. What kind of friendship could I offer when I was barely hanging on myself? Within five minutes of speaking to Julie, I realized there was no need to be hesitant; God indeed had purpose in crossing our paths. Julie and I bonded over the phone immediately, and once I met Ken I loved him just as much. Their son, Sam, is nothing short of amazing.

Ken and Gary were diagnosed with lung cancer the very same week. Ken was an athlete, a nonsmoker, and fifty-eight years old. If they chose to come to Bethany, their son, Sam, was going to be in Alec's class. The only difference between Gary's and Ken's cases was the type of cancer they had; not only that, but by the time they had found Ken's cancer it had left his lung and moved into his brain. This singular variable made all the difference in how Gary and Ken were treated.

Gary's lung was removed, while Ken's was not. Gary had four of the worst chemo treatments a body can handle and six-and-a-half weeks of radiation. Ken's treatment course was very different. He had twenty-two chemo treatments, two lung surgeries, two brain surgeries, ten days of radiation to his brain, and then eight more chemo treatments, which were a part of a trial procedure.

Julie and I kept in touch sporadically over the summer.

We were both neck-deep in dealing with cancer, and, as you can imagine, there was not a whole lot of time for coffee and get-to-know-you teas. Fortunately, Julie and I are both direct and transparent people, so we didn't have any problem getting "real" quickly. Cancer had linked our families like superglue—no typical warm-up time needed.

Since Ken and Gary were both diagnosed with cancer on the same week, we were on the same testing schedule. August of 2012 brought with it another all clear for Gary, but Ken's news was crushing. There was nothing else they could do for him—he was given anywhere between two weeks to two months to live. Needless to say, it was beyond heartbreaking. Gary and I both cried for our new friends. We were not beyond asking God, why?

Julie's response to their news in light of ours was amazing. She never bemoaned her own situation, and she didn't pull away from us; rather, she actually did the exact opposite. She pressed in and wanted us to share every step of our journey with them. I highly doubt I could have been so grace filled if the roles were reversed.

I took her through all the steps we had walked. As mature Christians, they were eager to apply all we discussed, especially praying Scripture out loud. We prayed together many, many times. We also brought in reinforcements. Jane and Mike Allison and Mary all came by and prayed for Ken as well. Ken came to chapel at Bethany and the students prayed for him with the sweetest of hearts. We persevered in the heavenly realms for his healing, asking God to touch him.

Ken and Julie were tireless in their search for a cure. They went to Chicago every three weeks for a trial procedure he was taking part in, while Sam stayed with us. To say the least, the trial was brutal—mentally, spiritually, and physically. Julie, on more than one occasion, thought that if cancer didn't get him, the treatments surely would. She believes to this day that the trial treatments promoted more suffering than necessary, but Ken still persevered.

September came and went, as did October, November, December, and January. The pain and suffering he endured was intolerable, yet his attitude stayed amazingly positive. He was contagiously confident in the Lord and steadfast in trusting God. He never for one moment conceded the opportunity for healing.

One afternoon in January of 2013, while sitting with Ken and Julie in their living room, Julie told me about a dream she had the night before. In the dream she saw her father and father-in-law, both of whom passed away a few years earlier, sitting on a porch swing waiting for Ken as he walked up the sidewalk. This dream gave Julie such peace as she was overcome with the love they displayed for Ken as they waited for him to walk up the sidewalk.

Ken didn't miss a beat as she told us of her dream. He said, "I'm glad they were sitting because they're going to have to wait a while longer. I'm not going home yet." We all chuckled. It was impossible not to be taken in by Ken's personality. We settled into our prayer positions, which usually consisted of Ken lying down on the couch, Julie kneeling on the floor at his head, and I typically sat down by his legs.

As we all began praying, all of a sudden Ken propped

himself up on one elbow, looked me straight in the eye, and said, "Rosey, how come Gary and not me?" I had no place to hide. I had no answer. I knew I had to honor his transparency with complete honesty though every part of me wanted to offer a solution I didn't have.

"Ken, I just don't know," I said. "I have been storming the gates of heaven with that same question myself for months. What I do know is that both you and Gary have spiritually responded the exact same way. You have both boldly and publically kept your eyes on the Lord. You have both been steadfast in your belief in God's will to heal."

I continued, "Ken, you have both loved Him with all your heart. There is amazing beauty in your faithfulness; there is pure power in your relationship with God. Your life screams to all of us about obedience in the face of adversity; love, and trust in the face of great suffering.

"Ken, you have shown us all that having a relationship with God goes beyond treating Him like Santa. You have shown us how to leave nothing on the table in our relationship with Him except His sovereignty. Through your example of faith you have helped so many people grow closer to God, including Gary and myself."

Ken's response was pure Ken: "Well, I'm still here so I'll keep asking," he assured us. Boy, could he make me laugh.

We prayed for a few more minutes and then I left. I could barely drive home for the tears that were streaming down my cheeks. My gut feeling about Julie's dream was that God was telling us Ken was about to go home. But Ken wasn't home yet, and that meant there was still more time to press in, but it would be increasingly difficult, especially as his physical state continued to deteriorate.

A week before Ken passed away, Julie called. "Rosey, I need to put Ken in hospice. We had hoped to keep him home, but I can't manage his care anymore. I just need to be his wife now, not his nurse."

"Oh, Julie, yes, that is exactly who you need to be," I replied.

"It's so hard," Julie said. "I feel like I need to be with him through this process. Will you stand in the gap for me and continue to pray for healing? I can't do both. I just can't. I can't pray for healing and walk him home at the same time."

"Yes, I will continue to pray," I assured her, "as will all those who love you. Go be with Ken. God knows your heart. He knows your suffering. He will surround you, Sam, and Ken with all that you need. He will be faithful to tenderly love you through this time."

I prayed with her and then hung up the phone. I supported Julie's personal decision to stop pressing in for healing because of something I had learned from my dear friend and coworker, Jean Figi, months earlier. On March 23, 2012, Jean lost Paul, her husband of over forty-five years, from complications due to diabetes.

There is no one like Jean Figi. She is a dynamo, a spiritual warrior, a ball of energy, wit, and more shenanigans than you can possibly imagine. When we worked together, she used to tease me that when she goes to heaven she's going to ask God to be my guardian angel so she can really have some fun. I love Jean. In fact, everyone does except perhaps late students looking for grace for being tardy.

Jean had helped her husband, Paul, through all the stages of diabetes. He was supposed to live five years, but he lived another fifteen. When he lost the use of his hands and feet, she stepped in and became his hands and feet for him. When he needed miracle cures for wounds that wouldn't heal, she sought our Father in heaven and they healed. She never wavered, so when she was sharing her heart with me shorty after Paul died, I had to sit up and listen, even if I was floored with her revelation.

"Rosey," she said to me one day, "I was so busy praying for healing and tending to Paul's needs, I wonder if I should have been less concerned about the details of healing and just sat with him and held his hand."

"Jean, you never left his side. What do you mean?" I said dumbfounded by her comment. She had been a tower of strength and support for him.

In true Jean fashion, she dismissed my drama with a wave of her hand and continued. "I know," she said, "I was there for him, but mentally I was occupied with his healing. Rarely was I just *there* for him. I wonder if he ever wanted to talk about his pending death, if he wanted to talk about what was happening. I know God never left his side. In fact, right before he died he looked at me and said, 'I'm healed,' but I wonder if I should have accepted his pending death at some point and just sat with him instead of always pressing in."

I had no words for my friend as she told me this; I just knew in my spirit that she spoke wisdom, wisdom that at some point in my journey I still might have needed myself. When Julie was telling me she needed to be at Ken's side, I supported her because of my previous conversation with Jean. After I hung up the phone with Julie, I got down on my knees. "Lord, please extravagantly love on this amazing family. Love them through their hour of despair. They are faithful witnesses of Your grace and glory. Jesus, this is so beyond my understanding, but I trust You, Lord. Please be with Ken, Julie, and Sam."

Ken went home to be with the Lord on February 18, 2013. We had the pleasure to know Ken in the worst and most heroic months of his life. He didn't just invite us into his home; he invited us into his life and in a very short time he left an indelible mark upon us.

At his funeral, Gary and I realized Ken made all people feel like they were his best friends. Ken was Ken to everyone he met—engaging, sincere, funny, empathetic, and simply charming. We accepted his death, yet honestly Ken's question of "why Gary and not me" haunted us. Gary and I went before the Lord many times to ask a very respectful, why?

We didn't ask in disobedience or in anger. We had accepted long ago the truth that the Lord's ways are often way above our understanding. We asked why with a sincere desire to understand God's purpose in the midst of all the suffering. "Lord, we know nothing is wasted in Your economy. How do You plan to advance the kingdom through the lives of Ken and Gary? Was it simply out of compassion that You had our paths cross, because You knew we needed each other's support? Or was there something more?"

It would not be beyond God's loving character to have our family's lives intersect simply because we were in need of each other. He is that generous, and He is that good. However, our friendship seemed more pregnant with purpose than just mere encouragement. Perhaps it was because we needed it to be. We needed this all to mean something more.

As Julie and Sam healed, we didn't see them as much—Sam and Alec were in the middle of acclimating to junior high and all that comes with it. Julie was adjusting to her new life and taking time to allow God to mend her broken heart. She had gone to a place that even at my most empathetic I simply couldn't enter. The only people to truly understand her pain are those who have also lost the love of their lives in a similar fashion. Through the whole process, Julie has remained an amazing witness to God's grace, but she will also tell you it has been a devastating journey.

THE REST OF THE STORY

It wasn't until the opportunity to write this book came along that God gave me the "rest of the story." He brought back to my memory Daniel and his friends, Shadrach, Meshach, and Abednego. He gently asked me to read this Scripture again. As I read Daniel 3 again, verses 16–18 jumped out at me:

> Shadrach, Meshach and Abednego replied to the king, "O Nebuchadnezzar, we do not need to defend ourselves before you in this matter. If we are thrown into the blazing furnace, the God we serve is able to save us from it, and he will rescue us from your hand, O king. But even if he does not, we want you to know, O king, that we will not serve your gods or worship the image of gold you have set up" (NIV).

I called Julie. "Julie, I think there was unseen purpose in Ken's death," I said to her after reading that passage of Scripture.

"What? Really? Do tell," she said. "Spill the beans."

"Well, I think as I tell Gary's story, Ken's story needs to be told as well. Ken's journey is the perfect example of what Shadrach, Meshach, and Abednego—Daniel's friends—said before the king. Do you remember that story?"

"Yes, I know the story, but where are you going with this?" she asked.

"Remember what they told the king? They said that whether or not God saved them, He was still God. Julie, their faith was fierce." I was covered in goose bumps.

I continued, "Gary and Ken's lives are a perfect example of this Scripture—start to finish. Shadrach, Meshach, and Abednego didn't want to have to endure the fire. But they wouldn't bow to the demands of Nebuchadnezzar either. This is the part Ken walked out so beautifully. He didn't bow to cancer. He stood against it with fierce faith, saying to us all that our job is to honor God regardless of our circumstances.

"We are to be obedient to all Scripture asks of us, walk in faith, storm the gates of heaven, and claim His sovereignty, whether or not we receive healing. Look at the impact Shadrach, Meshach, and Abednego made on King Nebuchadnezzar. Nebuchadnezzar began to praise God after they came out of the furnace. God is going to bring people closer to Himself through Ken's example of fierce, reckless faith!"

Julie was quiet for a moment before speaking. "I know He is," she said, then paused a moment. "Ken would love this."

She was quiet for a moment longer, then said, "He was so faithful, wasn't he, Rosey?"

"Ken's faith and obedience were amazing," I assured her with fresh tears rolling down my cheeks. "So were you…and so you continue to be."

"God had us completely cloaked in His presence," Julie said. "He really did. It was unbelievable. Even in my worst hours I could feel Him embracing me. You know, five days before Ken died he said something to me that was so profound. I wrote it down in my journal. Can I read it to you?"

"Of course."

"OK, here it is. As I was walking by his hospital bed in the living room one afternoon, collecting his lunch dishes, just a week before he died, out of nowhere he said to me, 'Always love me.' I really wished he had asked me something hard. That was like asking me to always breathe. It's a non-effort. I was born for both."

Julie continued, "Rosey, when he said this to me, he wasn't sad. He wasn't concerned about trying to tell me how to run the house. He was so joyful, he was so filled with love; love was the most important thing to him, and that was because he felt so loved by God. I felt Jesus holding onto both Ken and me, wrapping us both up in His arms."

"Your whole house was full of Jesus—we all felt it when we were there. Even though Ken was so sick, it never felt like an infirmary. You know, Julie, Ken left nothing on the table when asking for healing. He loved the Lord with reckless abandon yet he still went home. I think it's why people are afraid to hope in a God we can't control. We have to love Him completely surrendered and stand steadfast in belief like Ken. It's such a scary place to be."

I continued, "I think people are afraid to ask God for healing because what if illness takes a person home? They think they are not loved or not good enough or that they don't have enough faith. They don't want to be disappointed, so they don't ask, or barely ask, for healing.

"Julie, what Ken allowed us all to witness was an authentic relationship with our loving God. Ken trusted God enough to press Him hard but then say, 'All right, I guess I'm coming home, and, Lord, You're still on the throne.' I love that he wasn't concerned with earthly things for you and Sam. He even trusted God with your day-to-day details too." I laughed and then said, "But I bet you wished Ken left you a laundry list of at least a few things, right?"

"Seriously, Rosey," Julie said. "When I get to heaven, I'm going to give him a swift kick in the butt! Oddly though, trying to figure out all Ken used to do made me a stronger person. God even used my grief and confusion to say, 'You can do this; I'm right here.' God got me through even that minor stuff. He has been so faithful."

Then she said, "Write that book, Rosey. People need to understand that the Lord does not abandon His faithful, and they shouldn't be afraid to ask the Almighty to bless them with healing, because His grace is sufficient no matter the result."

"It's too bad we don't get to understand what that fully means until we walk through trials," I said. "God always heals; we just want Him to heal this side of heaven, don't we?"

"Yep, that's the truth and what we forget"—I picked up her

thought in midsentence—"is that His grace is sufficient," we said in unison.

"Rosey, I'm still cashing in on that truth every day because I'm a card-carrying member of the GGIS club!"

From the day of Gary's diagnosis in March of 2011 through the end of 2013, several of our friends and family have gone home to be with the Lord through the pathway of illness. Paul Figi, Norma Seabloom, Gary's uncle Ron Johnson, John Michelau, Sally Dale, and Greg's (Gary's older brother) wife, Sarah Wadsworth. Each of these people taught Gary and me how to battle with great confidence and trust God's nature as our shield.

God knows each one of His children to the very cells of our DNA. We can trust that He will assist us in our difficulties according to what we individually need. The trick is to love Him so recklessly in the process that we leave nothing on the table when asking for healing except His sovereignty.

Chapter 10

Recovery

In his kindness God called you to share in his eternal
glory by means of Christ Jesus. So after you have suffered
a little while, he will restore, support, and strengthen you,
and he will place you on a firm foundation
(1 Peter 5:10–11 NLT).

The months came and went and Gary stayed cancer free. He regained his strength, his weight, his confidence, and his mental state. Again, I wish it were as easy as just writing that sentence. In truth, however, he approached recovery like a true athlete, and through dedication and a daily routine he regained his strength back over time.

When you have only one lung, everything is infinitely harder. Gary was left with a continuous dull pain where the internal surgical cuts were made. He went back to running, but ultimately he said he didn't feel like his body liked it anymore so he switched to biking. He tried to get back on the ice rink and play some hockey, but one of the side effects of chemotherapy is a reaction in his hands and feet, where they go white in the cold and he loses all circulation. It's very painful.

The radiation scarred his esophagus so his throat is always scratchy. This makes him cough a lot, and when he coughs he can't breathe. The coughing fits are loud, painful, and violent.

Today his esophagus can cause him trouble if he talks too much or swallows the wrong way. He can no longer sing in the church choir or laugh really hard because these things cause a coughing spell. Dealing day to day with these adjustments is miniscule compared to the alternative, but they are adjustments just the same.

Gary also went through a phase where he was fearful cancer had returned. We have learned since that this is common in cancer survivors; we have also learned that the thought of cancer never really leaves you once you have went through something like this. I continue to pray that Gary will be completely released from the feeling that cancer could still be lurking around the corner—surely this isn't too big for God.

In August of 2013 Gary had his last six-month CT scan, so Dr. Leach said we could move to yearly scans now. He was also ecstatic when he told us that Gary had beaten down an extremely aggressive form of cancer. I asked about the potential of this being a remission stage. And he said, "This cancer doesn't have a remission state. It was going to win or Gary was—nothing in between."

Gary said, "Dr. Leach, you're good but we really know who healed me."

Dr. Leach just smiled. This time it was my turn to cry.

Gary and I went out to breakfast to celebrate the news. I finally told him all that he already knew but couldn't remember. We talked for such a long time. Gary was astounded. He wept, as did I. We sat in gratitude and disbelief, amazed how God had worked in our lives, ultimately healing Gary's body.

Many months later, when Bennett and Alec fully understood the odds of Gary's survival, they were more than a little irked that I had not been completely honest with them. They wished they had known the full truth. They are now seventeen and fourteen, so I can completely understand their point. They are becoming wonderful, strong, godly, and capable young men. It's hard for them to see themselves as anything but who they have become; plus, it's almost impossible for them to understand an Irish women's "she bear" instinct. However, I have a feeling that as they become parents themselves, they will achieve a greater understanding of my motivations.

Two years have passed since Ken went home to be with the Lord, and yet Julie and Sam continue to thrive. Sam has grown at least nine inches in that time, he has a special gift for theater, and he loves to participate in anything that involves music or singing. Julie just returned from a week in New York with Inheritance of Hope, an organization that gives families struggling with terminal cancer a vacation with other families in their same position. She, Ken, and Sam had used this service shortly after Ken was diagnosed. Now she was paying forward the love she received by helping other families who were in need.

Julie has gone back to school to be a Christian marriage and family counselor. Her humor is still deadpan and hysterical. She is always transparent, direct, beautiful, and as lively as ever. She is still quick to cry when she talks about Ken, but she said at least she can leave the house now without completely breaking down—so it's an improvement.

Last week, as I sat next to Julie in a Bethany prayer group, I remembered all my mental wonderings of the past. Here was

Julie living out the culmination of my worst-case scenarios. What I couldn't envision then but could purely see now was the power and faithfulness of God through the process.

Her strength and joy is impossible to manufacture. She has told me that living victorious in God doesn't mean you are full of strength and conquering all you encounter. Rather, living victoriously in God means you have surrendered every fiber of your being to Him, and in complete surrender you gain immeasurable strength.

It was not easy for Julie or Sam, but God continues to see them through their grief and into their new life. I like to think Ken is up there helping things along.

WALK IN YOUR HEALING

For Gary and me, healing his body was a circular endeavor. We believe that we are comprised of mind, body, spirit, intellect, will, emotion, spirit, and soul. When one area is sick, the whole system is thrown off. Therefore, we tried, to the best of our ability, to approach healing in all sectors, but cancer caught us completely off guard. And, honestly, where do you start? It was obvious from the very beginning that we were not only fighting cancer but we were fighting anxiety and fear as well.

Team Brausen was quick to come to our aid by sending us dozens of books on how to heal from terminal illness. Quickly we realized that we couldn't possibility read all the books, so I would simply pray first and ask for God's guidance as to what Gary needed, then skim through pages until something jumped out. It's not a perfect strategy, but hopefully you have figured out by now that because God runs my heart and life I trust Him to cover my backside. He never disappoints. Many members of Team Brausen also read books for us and highlighted all the important parts so it was easy for me to skim through them as well.

Our limited research provided three significant discoveries that resonated with both Gary and me: exercise, the spice turmeric, and eliminating refined sugar.

EXERCISE

For Gary, exercise, no matter how much or how little, did amazing things for his mental health as well as for his body. His approach was to do something physical every day according to what he was capable of doing. During the third chemo treatment we found out that biking was like manna sent from heaven. His whole attitude changed. This was a no-brainer for Gary, but it's not for everyone. The best rule of thumb is to pray about it, take an honest assessment of your ability, and discuss exercise options with your doctor. If you are still going through treatments, it might be wise to wait until you have regained some strength before beginning to exercise on a regular basis.

TURMERIC SPICE

Early in our journey, our neighbor Kathy dropped by the book *Anticancer* by David Servan Schreiber, MD. Kathy is a women built for research. She is one of the most well-read people I know. When she gave me this book, I knew that it was important and I read it cover to cover.

This is where I first learned of the cancer-fighting properties of turmeric spice. In India, with all their pollution and active cigarette smoking, you would think they would have one of the highest occurrences of lung cancer in the world, and yet the opposite is true. They also have one of the lowest instances of Alzheimer's. When I read that there could be a possible link to low lung cancer rates because of the prolific use of the spice turmeric in their diets, my heart leapt up in my chest.

Such a physical response usually means that the Lord wants me to pay attention to what is going on around me, or to what I am reading. Apparently, when turmeric is heated, its cancer fighting power grows by 2,000 percent. As soon as chemotherapy ended, Gary began making himself turmeric tea every morning. He mixes a half-teaspoon into boiling water, he adds a dash of cayenne pepper, and sips it throughout the morning. Sometimes, I join him in this simple ritual, but mostly the kids and I take a turmeric supplement daily. Gary still drinks his tea every morning. The kids and I are not above teasing him just a little when it stains his lips yellow. He takes it all in stride .

REFINED SUGAR

There is a lot of data on refined sugar and the problems it can cause in the health and well-being of our body. Some doctors will say that this is still soft science, and perhaps this is true. Additional research still needs to be done, so this may take a while before the medical community at large takes a serious look at sugar.

Gary, however, felt very strongly that refined sugar was a culprit in sabotaging his recovery, so he went to an 80/20 philosophy. Eighty percent of the time he would say no to refined sugar and 20 percent of the time he allows himself a little treat.

CELERY

Finally, when Gary was asking the Lord what else his body needed to fight cancer, Gary heard the word *celery*. I looked up its benefits, and, sure enough, it is full of apigenin, a cancer fighter as well.[8] Gary still eats two or three stalks a day. We also went through a period of time when Gary would eat four teaspoons of pureed asparagus daily. But as soon as he felt like this was no longer necessary, he stopped.

ORGANIC FOODS

As a basic rule of thumb, our whole family eats organically now. We try to avoid products that are not all natural—from our meat to our chicken to our vegetables and fruit. This can be expensive, so we have been very thankful that Costco has grown their organic and all natural sections exponentially over the last few years.

Though this has been based on our limited research, Gary and I have felt like it was important in Gary's fight against cancer. I would encourage you to find some good books, do your own research, and stick to what the Lord is showing you.

---

8   Sanjeev Shukla and Sanjay Gupta, "Apigenin: A Promising Molecule for Cancer Prevention," PMC, US National Library of Medicine, National Institutes of Heath, www.ncbi.nlm.nih.gov/pmc/articles/PMC2874462/, accessed 3/25/2015.

Chapter 11

Healing Is Complete, but God Isn't Done

Each of you should use whatever gift you have
received to serve others, as faithful stewards of
God's grace in its various forms (1 Peter 4:10 NIV).

When Gary was first diagnosed with cancer, our neighbor Mark asked Gary how he was going to live out the rest of his days, but, honestly, entertaining anything beyond getting through the current day seemed like an impossibility. God is not wasteful. Everything Gary learned through his journey is now being employed helping other victims of lung cancer. He has spent hours encouraging other cancer patients on the phone, in the chemotherapy infusion room, or just taking someone who is suffering for a much-needed walk. At first his desire to help came out of a good dose of survivor's guilt, but as time has passed, he sees the hope his victory gives others. His example is vital to those who need to see that it is possible to beat cancer. Gary often said while he battled his own illness that all he wanted to hear about were stories of success against cancer.

Being an ambassador to those who are currently suffering

is Gary's heart, but being obedient to the call did not come easy for Gary. He himself was not out of the woods the first time he visited with another lung cancer patient. The patient was his uncle Ron and he was in hospice. Can you imagine visiting a loved one who is dying of the very disease that you are still battling? For Gary it was almost an impossible task. He likes to tell everyone that the only reason he made it into the hospice room that day was because he married a feisty Irish women with pointy boots who does not tolerate excuses. I like to believe that I tried several approaches before I put my foot down, but all the boys laugh when I take this approach, so maybe there is some truth to Gary's version. Gary had nothing to be afraid of since Ron's first words when he saw him were, "Wow, you look good." The boys played the piano for Ron and we laughed and reminisced for quite some time. That visit was the first hard step into his ambassador ministry.

God also has him "shaking hands and kissing babies" with whoever will listen. If it increases awareness of lung cancer, increases funding to this horribly underfunded disease, and/or makes inroads for early detection, Gary is on board. He became a board member for the A Breath of Hope Lung Foundation in June of 2014.

Here is why Gary is so passionate for raising money and bringing awareness to lung cancer. The American Lung Association and A Breath of Hope Lung Foundation give some intriguing statistics that we would all do well to ponder:[9]

---

9   "Lung Cancer Fact Sheet," American Lung Association, http://www.lung.org /lung-disease/lung-cancer/resources/facts-figures/lung-cancer-fact-sheet .html#1, accessed January 19, 2015.

- Lung cancer is the leading cancer killer in both men and women in the United States. In 1987, it surpassed breast cancer to become the leading cause of cancer deaths in women as well. Lung cancer currently kills twice as many women as breast cancer.

- Lung cancer causes more deaths than the next three most common cancers combined (colon, breast, and pancreatic cancer). An estimated 159,260 Americans are expected to die from lung cancer in 2014, accounting for approximately 27 percent of all cancer deaths.

- The lung cancer five-year survival rate is lower than many other leading cancer sites (17.8 percent), such as the colon (65.4 percent), the breast (90.5 percent) and prostate (99.6 percent).

- Over half of people with lung cancer die within one year of being diagnosed.

- Lung cancer is underfunded because of the stigma of smoking. Lung cancer receives just $1,442 in federal research funding per death compared with $26,398 for breast cancer.

- Half of those diagnosed each year are nonsmokers—either those who have never smoked or former smokers. One in five women diagnosed with lung cancer never smoked.

THE WHITE RIBBON RIDE IS BORN

In December of 2013, Gary was having a really good talk with God in the shower when he suddenly felt inspired to begin a bike event for lung cancer. This wasn't going to be a small endeavor—he was inspired to go from Minneapolis to Duluth, which is a hundred and fifty mile trek.

He was so excited about his inspiration that he came bounding down the stairs into the kitchen: "Rosey, God just told me I should start a bike event to raise funds for lung cancer. I'm thinking a hundred and fifty miles from here to Duluth."

"Wow, really?" I said. "That's a pretty long way. Are you sure you can ride one hundred and fifty miles with one lung? Maybe the one hundred and fifty mile part was you. Maybe God was saying fifty miles instead," I replied skeptically.

"No, I heard one hundred fifty miles," he enthusiastically persisted. "Wouldn't that be something? I bet eventually we could raise a lot of money for lung cancer."

I wish I could say I was 100 percent behind him, but I had my doubts. I didn't have a doubt that God inspired him; my doubt was centered on whether or not he should be included

Family picture before bike event.

among the riders. My hesitation didn't matter, however, because Gary had heard God and there was no going back. He gathered a group of his buddies together, they designed a logo, mapped out a course, and gathered twenty dear friends and three volunteers for the maiden ride.

Many times I sought the Lord for wisdom about this bike event for Gary. God was always quiet on the topic; instead, He just blessed us with sign after sign, most of which happened on the ride itself.

It was going to be a two-day trip, seventy-five miles per day with food and water stops every ten to fifteen miles. Gary, Bennett, Alec, and I trained all summer. I began to feel better and better about the ride as Gary's stamina increased. My only concern was that he never actually rode seventy-five miles in one day, and certainly never seventy-five miles two days in a row.

The ride was scheduled for Saturday, August 2, 2014. God provided a beautiful weekend, the kind that makes Minnesotans say, "Now this is why we live here." I ended up being a part of the volunteer support team, so nineteen riders headed out.

Right from the beginning, God began to bless the ride from the beautiful weather to the many people we ran into who had lost someone to lung cancer. Here are some of my favorite God stories from the trip.

When we stopped in Hinckley, a woman named Gretchen gave us $100, which was her gambling money. Instead of going to the casino, she felt inspired to give it for lung cancer.

Gary went inside to use the bathroom of the VFW in Rush

City. When he exited there were a few folks gathered by the door admiring the middle-age man in spandex shorts. They were very friendly but a little rough around the edges. As Gary explained what he was up to, each of them one by one dropped their cigarettes to the ground and squished them out with their foot.

Though we didn't know it at the time, God had us pull over unexpectedly at an undesignated stop. This stop was at the end of long country road in the middle of nowhere, right before we got into the town of Hinckley. While I was stopped, the two lead bikers riding at a very fast pace were in need of water and food. They would have made it the rest of the way but I was glad we were there. Quietly, I asked God if we should go, and His response was not yet. A couple more riders came through, and they were all happy for the unexpected stop and cold water. Again, I asked if I should go. And again, "Not yet," was my answer. We started to pack up when a motorcyclist came up alongside us. He and his friend had stopped to have a cigarette.

I was giggling to myself as we walked up to greet each other. When we met, he asked what I was doing on the side of the road. I started laughing and asked him if he really wanted to know; and needless to say, he was a little freaked out but not enough to give up smoking. I gave him a card for the Breath of Hope website and told him there are no coincidences. (You must love him very much, Lord, for such a special appointment.)

While waiting at stop number two on the second day, I met a group of seniors in the small town of Finlayson. Four out of nine of these seniors had lost someone to lung cancer.

They waited to meet Gary and promised to start following the Breath of Hope website. Gary was happy to oblige, as he was completely in his element among these seniors.

In the middle of the second day we ran into a rainstorm of mega proportions. Again, God had me go slightly off course and stop at a shelter in Carlton. Two minutes after I pulled into the shelter, the three lead bikers pulled in as well. They were an hour ahead of schedule because they rode through their last stop. They had been riding in the rain for two hours and were now freezing and hungry. Thankfully, I had blankets in the car so they had a chance to warm up.

I returned to the original stopping point and waited for the others. All the bikers came in completely drenched, having ridden through the same storm. Gary, our friends Ken and Scott, and brother-in-law Kemper were in the last group, lagging an hour and a half behind. They never hit the rain and were shocked that everyone else was so soaked. Gary still says to this day that he would not have been able to complete the ride had he been drenched and chilled as well. He was already riding beyond his capacity.

At the end of the Munger Trail, all the bikers waited for Gary, Ken, Scott, and Kemper because they wanted Gary to lead them to the finish line. As we waited, a woman drove up to meet us. She had seen our colorful jerseys from her house up on the hill, and she loved the color so much she just had to come down and see what we were up to.

As I told her about the cause, the

Gary at the bike event.

expression on her face changed dramatically. I apologized for being too pushy and explained why I was so passionate about lung cancer and Gary's story. She proceeded to tell me that she had lost her husband to lung cancer two years earlier and had just moved back to Minnesota. As I looked at her, my heart filled with compassion. I told her that God isn't in the coincidence business; He has a plan for every encounter we have if we are willing to listen. She looked at me dumbfounded, took a card for the A Breath of Hope Lung Foundation website (www.abreathofhope.org), and said she would see us next year. She just happened to be an avid biker too.

Unfortunately, everyone did not come through the bike event unscathed. Our dear friend Mark had a horrible spill and severely broke his scapula in two places and a couple of ribs. We are thankful that it wasn't worse, but for Mark he had to endure months of recovery. Next year he gets a free jersey.

All together we raised about $4,000 for lung cancer. As a group, we decided that we would take sixty riders the following year and hope to raise between $16,000–$20,000. If God still wants us to chair this event, we will open it to the public. The MS society hosts a ride called the MS150 along this same course. With over 3,800 riders, they raised over $3 million. Gary gets excited when he thinks of the possibilities. We will see what God has up His sleeve.

LUNG CANCER SYMPOSIUM

The day after Gary's August 2014 appointment, he received a call from Dr. Leach. This surprised Gary immensely since he had never received a direct call from him before. Gary's first thought was, *Oh no. Did they miss something on my chest CT scan?* He cautiously asked Dr. Leach why he was calling and if something was wrong.

Dr. Leach burst into his very infectious laugh and said. "Absolutely not. I am wondering if you would be willing to speak at the Lung Cancer Symposium in October." Gary was deeply honored and agreed to speak.

At the Lung Cancer Symposium, after a heartfelt and tearful introduction by Dr. Leach, and with Julie Hull at our table, in front of a hundred plus doctors from pathologists to surgeons, Gary shared his story.

As Gary spoke, I looked around the room at all the people who have dedicated their lives to helping people overcome lung cancer. To me they are all warriors, frontline heroes who dedicate their lives to those suffering from lung cancer, hoping for an opportunity to decrease an 84 percent fatality rate. I was touched at how important Gary's story was to them; they also need hope and inspiration because God does work healing through their hands as well as through the prayers of people.

After the symposium, Gary's entire medical team all convened together. It had been almost three years since we had seen many of them. Dr. Graczyk, Jody, and I talked about how difficult it is for them to be the messenger of heartbreaking news. We also discussed the burden they had carried for us as Gary battled through chemo and radiation. They said that every single doctor who saw Gary's final pathology report thought Gary's case was terminal.

On the way home, Gary and I reminisced about how God drew us closer to Himself through the journey of cancer. We marveled at His kindness and mercies that were new every day. We wept with gratitude for Team Brausen, and we wept for the return of normalcy. Yes, God is truly good indeed. This is why the psalmist cries out,

> Give thanks to the LORD, for he is good! His love endures forever. Has the LORD redeemed you? Then speak out! Tell others he has redeemed you from your enemies (Psalm 107:1–2 NLT).

Chapter 12

Give God
Your Heart

At first glance, this is a feel-good story of hope in the face of terminal illness. But what we pray you have discovered is the truth that God's greatest and singular desire is to have a relationship with you that is intimate, real, and tangible. And through your relationship with Him you will be healed, whether that healing needs to take place emotionally, spiritually, or physically.

God longs to answer your questions, calm your fears, and show you His unlimited, unconditional love. He wants to lavishly bless you with His presence and call you His beloved. He wants to break out of the boundaries of religion or church and take up residence in your heart. He wants you to know that our supernatural is His natural and that nothing is beyond His ability to overcome. He wants you to call on Him so He can teach you to hear His voice. He wants to fulfill the promise of Psalm 91:14–16:

Because he has loved Me, therefore I will deliver him;
I will set him securely on high, because he has known
My name. He will call upon Me, and I will answer him;

I will be with him in trouble; I will rescue him and honor him. With a long life I will satisfy him and let him see My salvation.

I would encourage you to read this verse again out loud, but this time substitute your own name every time you see the pronoun "he" or "him." These are God's words written specifically for you. Look at how He describes His nature throughout this Scripture. He longs to rescue, protect, deliver, honor, satisfy, and show you His salvation. All you have to do is love Him and acknowledge His name. It's beautifully simple and more complicated than anyone ever dreamed, but take heart: He loves it when you try—not when you are perfect but when you honestly try. There is no further explanation that is needed. He loves our hearts, and His love is complete. Who needs anything more?

We hope you look beyond the miracle of Gary's healing and into the real truth and miracle that the great I AM longs to meet you in your heart too. His greatest desire is not for you to live through our experience but to trust Him with all of your heart. He also longs for you to walk with Him sooner, rather than later. This was Gary's one regret—he wishes He had heeded the call of God on his life long before cancer moved in as a houseguest.

It's beyond amazing, but the God of the universe wants to meet you exactly where you're at today, not when you are all cleaned up and perfect. He wants you just as you are. Take a look at your schedule, because I can guarantee you don't have anything more important than getting on your knees right now and giving Him your heart. This is why Jesus says, "Behold, I stand at the door and knock; if anyone hears My voice and opens the door, I will come in to him and will dine with him, and he with Me" (Revelation 3:20).

Remember, God always heals.

Gary, Bennett, Alec, and I will be faithful to pray for your journey.

Alec, Rosey, Gary, and Bennett, October 2014,
two months after Gary received the "all clear."

Our Steps to Healing

1. Seek the Lord. Go to the Lord ASAP ask Him to make your path clear. Pour out your heart to Him, ask Him to heal you, and ask Him the way you should go.

2. Read all the healings recorded in the Bible. Which stories stand out to you? Meditate on those stories and ask God to reveal their importance to your situation.

3. Find a book that contains a list of God's promises in the Bible. (See *All God's Promises* by BroadStreet Publishing). Say the Scriptures that meet your current need out loud over yourself or your loved one. These promises are typically organized by category for ease.

4. Ask your friends and family to pray. Keep them updated as your situation changes. Remember this is not a burden for others. They want to help. It is actually a privilege. Gather them together for group prayer whenever possible.

5. Be transparent and spend time in repentance. Ask the Holy Spirit to bring any sin to your memory

so you can repent. After you have gone through repentance, it is very important to receive God's forgiveness and let your icky stuff go. It is not our Lord's nature to want you to feel guilt or shame; those are tools of the enemy.

6. Put on your spiritual armor every day. Pray Ephesians 6:10–18 and ask Jesus to cover your mind, body, spirit, will, emotion, and soul in His shed blood.

7. Be aware of your thoughts and what you profess with your words. If they do not follow a Christ-like pattern, they aren't worth saying or thinking.

8. Walk in gratitude for the healing you have already received and then walk it out to the best of your ability. Remember healing can be instantaneous but it also can take a while. Remind yourself that God's will is to heal our diseases and bind our wounds (Jeremiah 30:17).

9. Laugh as much as possible and continue to make plans for tomorrow and the future.

10. Then stand until you have victory.

Healing Scriptures

After Gary regained his full health, I explored more healing Scriptures in the Bible. There are many, many sites on the Internet that confirm what God was speaking into my spirit, plus so many scriptures about healing!

One site that I found as I was completing this book made me smile from ear to ear. It's www.prayingscriptures.com. I love this site because it is so simple and many of the Scriptures the Holy Spirit brought Gary and I are listed there. Plus it also speaks of the importance of speaking Scripture out loud over yourself.

When I found the site it was further confirmation about God's nature. He always confirms Himself through Scripture.

Here are Scriptures we encourage you to pray out loud over yourself and your loved ones for whatever need you have.

Galatians 3:13. Christ has redeemed us from the curse of the law, having become a curse for us.

1 Peter 2:24. [Jesus] bore our sins in His own body on the tree, that we, having died to sins, might live for righteousness—by whose stripes you were healed.

Isaiah 53:5. He was wounded for our transgressions, He was bruised for our iniquities; the chastisement for our peace was upon Him, and by His stripes we are healed.

Matthew 8:17. He Himself took our infirmities and bore our sicknesses.

Psalm 107:20. He sent His word and healed them, and delivered them from their destructions.

Proverbs 3:7. Do not be wise in your own eyes: fear the Lord and depart from evil.

Proverbs 3:8. [Fearing the Lord and departing from evil] will be health to your flesh, and strength to your bones.

Exodus 15:26. I am the Lord who heals you.

Psalm 103:3. Bless the Lord, O my soul, And forget not all His benefits: Who forgives all your iniquities, Who heals all your diseases, Who redeems your life from destruction, Who crowns you with lovingkindness and tender mercies, Who satisfies your mouth with good things, So that your youth is renewed like the eagle's.

Exodus 23:25. Serve the Lord your God, and He will bless your bread and your water. And I will take sickness away from the midst of you.

Proverbs 16:24. Pleasant words are like a honeycomb, sweetness to the soul and health to the bones.

Isaiah 58:8. Your light shall break forth like the morning, your healing shall spring forth speedily, and your righteousness shall go before you; the glory of the Lord shall be your rear guard.

Psalm 118:17. I shall not die, but live, and declare the works of the Lord.

Psalm 147:3. He heals the brokenhearted and binds up their wounds.

Proverbs 17:22. A merry heart does good, like a medicine, but a broken spirit dries the bones.

3 John 2. Beloved, I pray that you may prosper in all things and be in health, just as your soul prospers.

Mark 16:17. These signs will follow those who believe: In My name they will cast out demons; they will speak with new tongues; ...they will lay hands on the sick, and they will recover.

James 5:15. The prayer of faith will save the sick, and the Lord will raise him up. And if he has committed sins, he will be forgiven.

James 5:16. Confess your trespasses to one another, and pray for one another, that you may be healed.

Matthew 8:13. Go your way; and as you have believed, so let it be done for you.

Prayer List for Repentance

The Holy Spirit knows which sins should be repented of first. I am often surprised when He wants to heal me of what I think is a smaller sin before tackling my bigger stuff. Pray and ask for His guidance before you begin repentance. Then wait for Him to bring memories back to your mind. If this is difficult, use this guide below. If possible, Scripture tells us to repent to one another. If this is too difficult for you to do, then realize it is more important to get started. God will either bring someone into your life whom you can trust or He will heal your potential trust issues.

As God shows you the sin He wants you to confess, follow the next few steps.

1. Ask God to forgive you for participating in that particular sin.
2. Ask Him to forgive any other participants in that sin memory.
3. Give forgiveness to anyone who caused you pain or suffering.

4. Accept and receive God's forgiveness for yourself.
5. Thank God according to Scripture that He will remember your sin no more for His own sake. Isaiah 43:25 says, "I, even I, am he who blots out your transgressions, for my own sake, and remembers your sins no more."
6. Ask God through His Holy Spirit to alert you when you are committing this sin again.
7. If you are reminded of sins that you have already repented of, speak out loud, "I remember that I have forgiven myself and all parties involved in this memory. Thank you, God that I have received your forgiveness, and I no longer have to carry this memory around."

If you're struggling to know what to pray for, below is a list of sins we as humans fall into along with questions God may use to search you heart.

JEALOUSY, ENVY

- Have you ever wished to be more like someone else?
- Have you wished for the attention someone else received?
- Have you felt like you have been overlooked when someone else received all the glory or recognition?

CRITICAL ATTITUDE

- Have you thought you could do something better than another?

- Have you judged someone else's work performance, financial decisions, parenting, attitude, clothing choice, or behavior?
- Have you judged someone's heart by assuming they are thoughtless or clueless?

UNFORGIVENESS, GRUDGES, BITTER ROOTS

- Do you have memories that bring you pain and anger?
- Have you ever said, "I will never forget when so and so did 'this' to me?"
- Do you harbor ill will towards anyone?
- Do you keep past hurts alive by reliving them in your memory?

SELF-LOATHING, SELF-PITY, BEING A VICTIM

- Do you wish you looked different?
- Do you wish you could change a physical feature of your body?
- Do you believe the voices in your head when they say you are different, weird, isolated, or forgotten?
- Do you say "I hate myself" or I'm so stupid"?

GOSSIP

- Do you talk poorly of others?
- In order to gain ground in a social setting, do you air others peoples mistakes?
- Do you delight in passing on "news" of other people's business?

SELFISHNESS

- Are you overly preoccupied with your own needs?
- Do you only help others when it is convenient for you?
- Are you always aware of how you would benefit from any given action or interaction?

GREED

- Do you hold onto money as security?
- Do you feel resentful when giving?
- Do you negotiate with God about giving?

LUST

- Have you participated in chat rooms, pornography, strip clubs?
- Have you flirted with another outside of marriage?
- Have you looked at someone outside of marriage and imagined being with him or her?

PRIDE

- Do you have trouble asking for help?
- Do you have trouble saying I'm sorry?
- Do you think that you are usually right?
- Have you felt superior to others for a God-given gift you did nothing to earn? For example, your intellect, temperament, social skills, athleticism, looks.

Acknowledgements

This book would be another three chapters long if I truly was able to thank all who walked us through this journey, and even then I wouldn't do justice to the kindness we received.

Team Brausen, I remember each and every act of kindness you bestowed on my little family—from Lynn's homemade matzo ball soup, Chris who painstakingly kept Gary's car running, Bill who cleared our house of rodents that were eating our air condition wires, Cindy and Trudi who helped me get ready for "what" we didn't know, Sarah and Jean who lovingly set up a meal plan when I was most resistant, and every act of kindness in between. We are so very thankful. Gary's healing and the publication of this book is really your victory. None of it would have been possible without your prayers and support.

Pete, Tom, and Joe. I love being the sister nestled between the bro-pack even if you are the reason for my sophomoric sense of humor. (You are now officially in the book.) Pete, thank you for saying you wouldn't want to be me at the pearly gates if I didn't at least try to write our story. You have very successfully mastered Dad's raised eyebrow look.

Norma, Gary and I will never forget your mentorship during our darkest days even while you battled cancer yourself. Your faith without fanfare is legendary. Your last piece of advice to always love one another still rings in my ears. I love envisioning you kicking your heels up in heaven.

Carlton, David, Ryan, and the rest of the publishing team, thank you for listening to the prompting of the Holy Spirit and turning our story into a book. We couldn't have had a more encouraging, prayerful team. David, thank you for teaching me through your book *Write Your Book* the craft of writing our story for others to read. Without your experience, wisdom, encouragement, and guidance, not one word of this story would have ever made it onto an actual page.

To our medical team, Joe, Matt, Jody, Brynn, Mark, and Laura, you will always hold a privileged position in our hearts. Thank you for your service to all who suffer.

Sweet Gary, I hope you know that this book would not have been possible without your willingness to be completely transparent and forthcoming about your journey. Through your honesty, humility, and courage others will have an opportunity to be real with our most precious God. Your teachable spirit has helped me to remember that I will always be a student of our Lord and that we will never come to the end of His love, mercy, and grace. Thank you for giving me all those books on writing when we were first married and then reminding me off and on for the past twenty years that I had not used your presents yet. Your faith insisting this story should be told has been unfaltering. And I love how you can still rock your jeans!

Father God, Mighty Lord, and precious Holy Spirit, it is by Your faithfulness that You built our faith. Where did our hope come from? It came from the Lord! Lord, I pray You will use this story to draw others into deeper relationship with You, and into healings of all types. Please Lord, dazzle them with Your godliness, satisfy their hunger, comfort them with Your limitless love, hide them in the shadow of Your wings, and let the love that You abundantly bestowed on my family bring hope to the hopeless. Thank You for letting us serve You through the telling of this story. Thank You, Jesus for the protection of Your shed blood and your gift of peace that can never be removed. We love who You are—completely and wholly God. You are so very good.